KAMOME SHIRAHAMA

Witch Hat Atelier

VOLUME

1

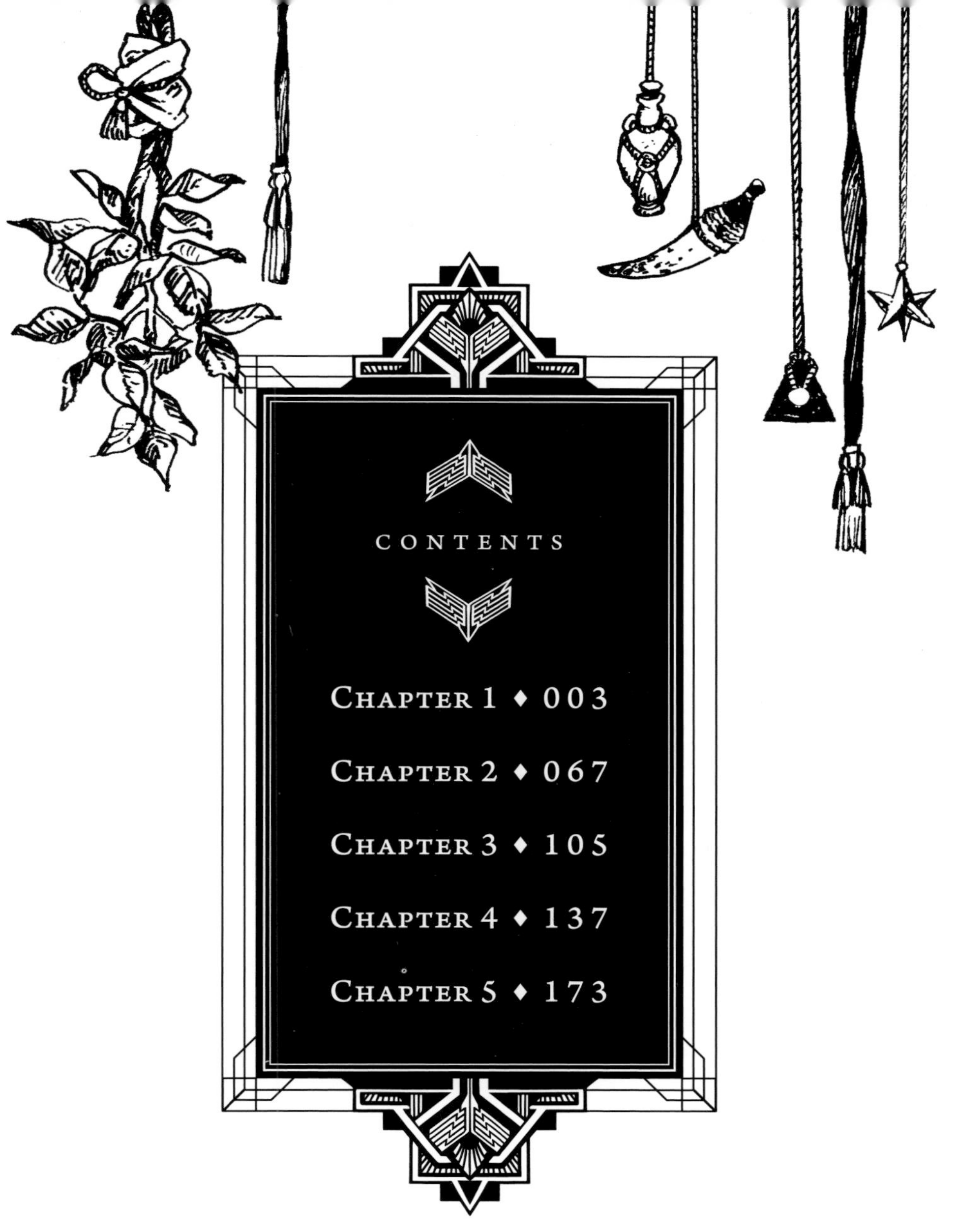

CONTENTS

Chapter 1 ♦ 003

Chapter 2 ♦ 067

Chapter 3 ♦ 105

Chapter 4 ♦ 137

Chapter 5 ♦ 173

WITCH HAT ATELIER

♦

KAMOME
SHIRAHAMA

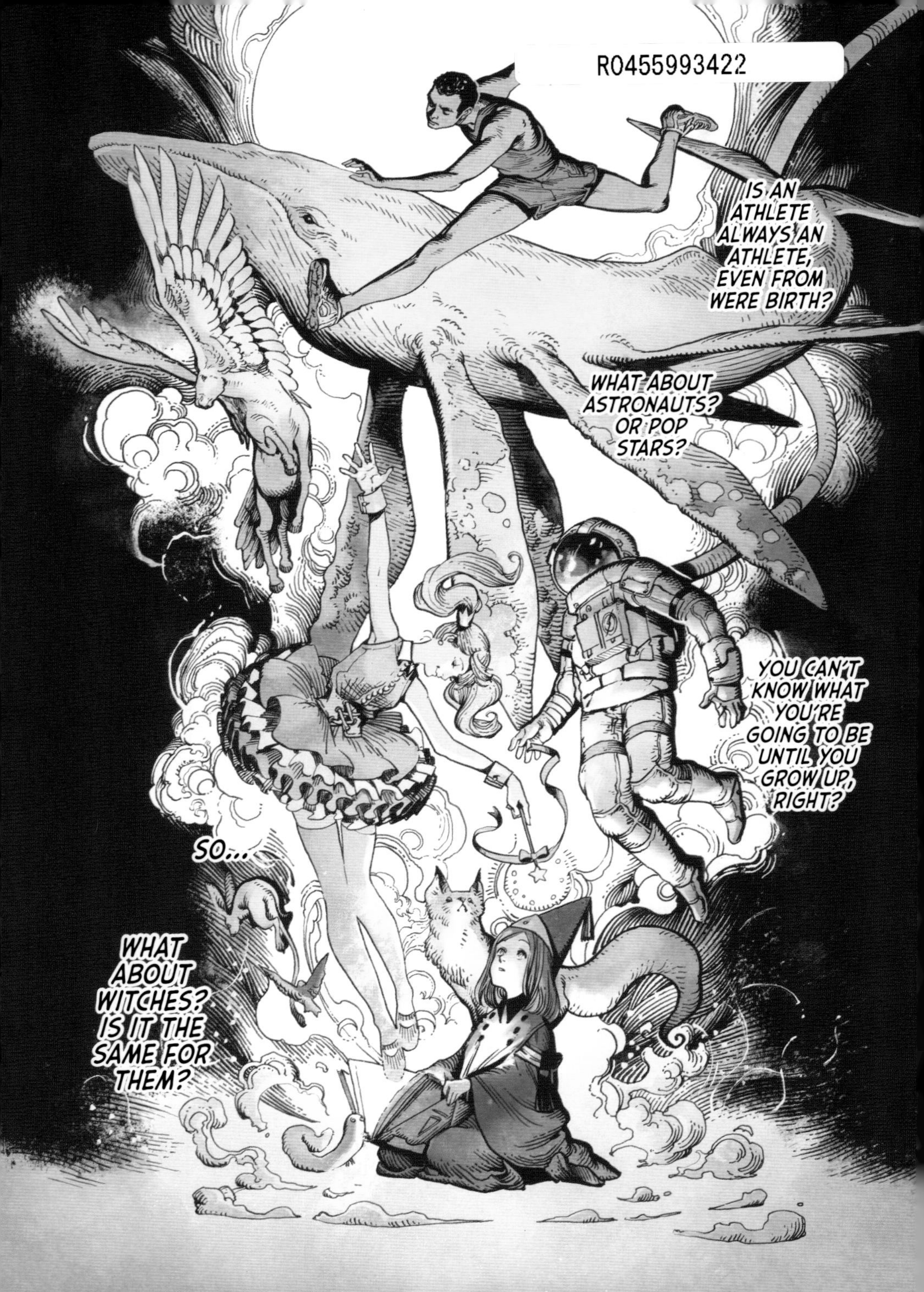
IS AN ATHLETE ALWAYS AN ATHLETE, EVEN FROM WERE BIRTH?
WHAT ABOUT ASTRONAUTS? OR POP STARS?
YOU CAN'T KNOW WHAT YOU'RE GOING TO BE UNTIL YOU GROW UP, RIGHT?
SO...
WHAT ABOUT WITCHES? IS IT THE SAME FOR THEM?

Chapter 1

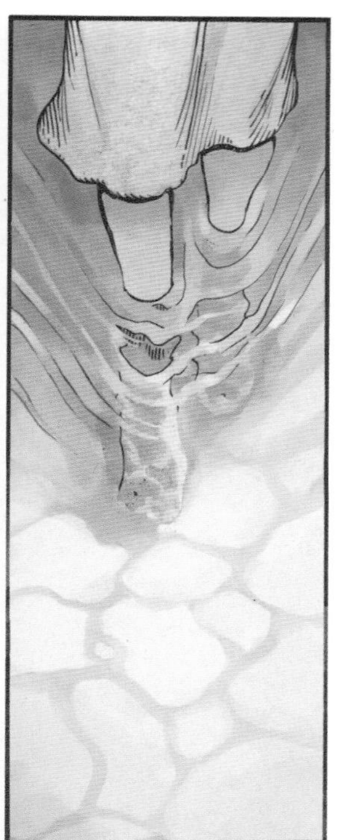

ミちばあーっ
SPLORSH

ざっぱ
SCRUB
ざっぱ
SCRUB
SCRUB
ざっぱ
SCRUB
ざっぱ
BUBBLE BUBBLE
あわあわ
FOAM
もこもこ
FOAM
じんわ
OOZE

OH!
SORRY ABOUT THE MESS!

DON'T WORRY. IT'LL BE GONE IN NO TIME.
THIS IS A MAGIC SPRING, YOU KNOW!

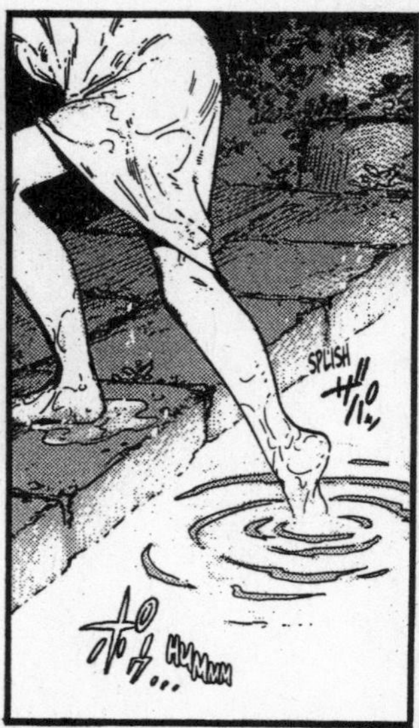
SPLISH
HUMMM

SHIIIINE

PERK
SO BEAUTIFUL ...
IT NEVER GETS OLD. MAGIC IS AMAZING!

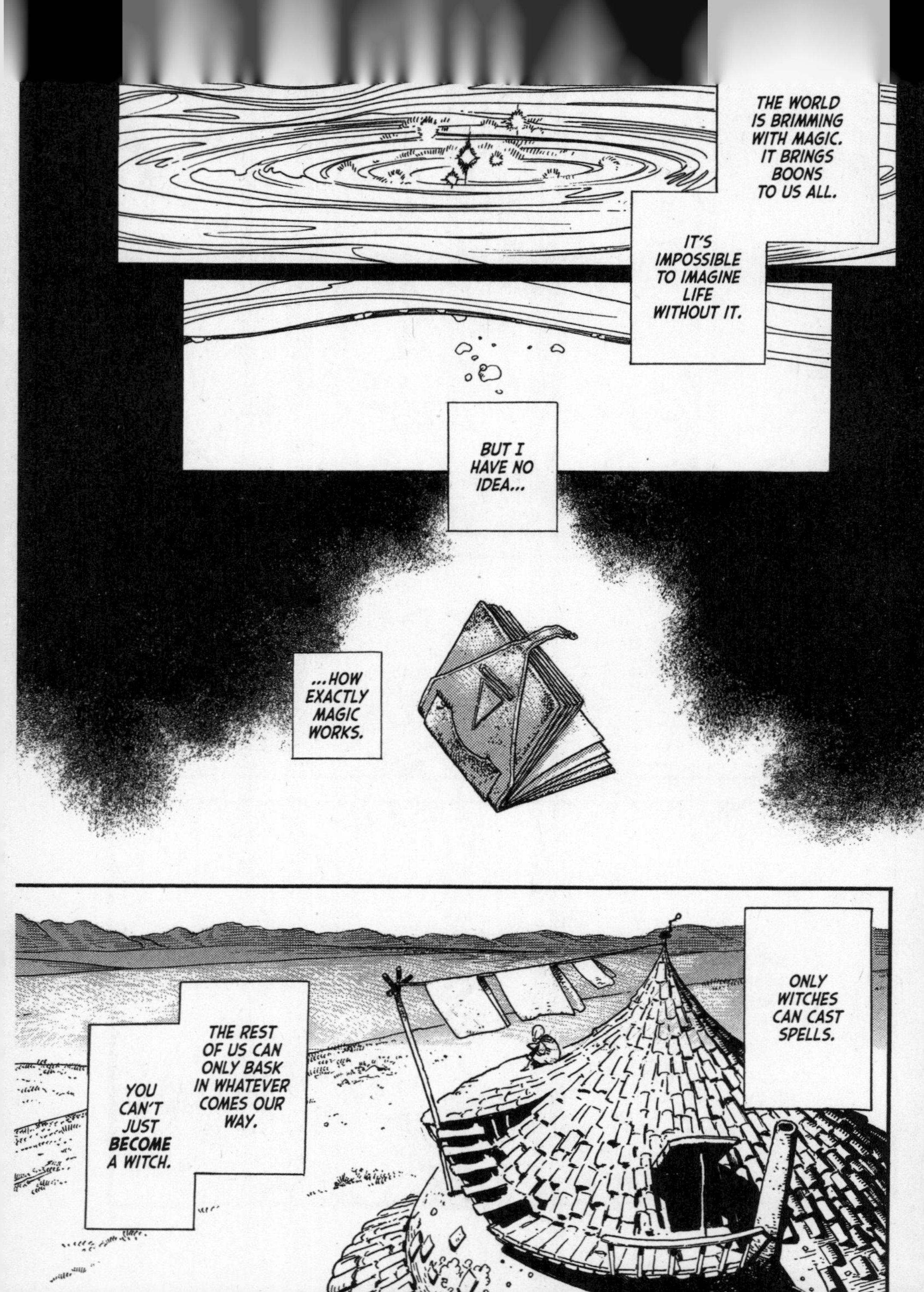
THE WORLD IS BRIMMING WITH MAGIC. IT BRINGS BOONS TO US ALL.
IT'S IMPOSSIBLE TO IMAGINE LIFE WITHOUT IT.
BUT I HAVE NO IDEA...
...HOW EXACTLY MAGIC WORKS.
ONLY WITCHES CAN CAST SPELLS.
THE REST OF US CAN ONLY BASK IN WHATEVER COMES OUR WAY.
YOU CAN'T JUST BECOME A WITCH.

GLANCE

I WISH...
...I HAD BEEN BORN A WITCH.

O, FRESHLY WASHED SHEET, CLEAN AND WHITE...

I COMMAND YOU NOW—BE MY CLOAK OF FLIGHT!
FW
IP

HANG
…

BLUSH
カァーーッ

HUH?!
ぶ
FWOOSH
わさーーッ

NO! DON'T GET CAUGHT IN THE WIND!
Wait! Stop!!
THAT'S NOT THE KIND OF FLYING I WAS TALKING ABOUT!!

…!
IS THAT A…?

TH-THUMP
THUMP

HFF...
HFF!

IT IS! IT'S A PEGASUS CARRIAGE!

I DON'T BELIEVE IT!
IT LANDED HERE IN THE VILLAGE!

I'VE NEVER SEEN A PEGASUS CARRIAGE TOUCH DOWN BEFORE!

MOM! MOM! LOOK OUTSIDE!

MOOO-OOM!

MOM, WHERE ARE YOU?
WHOA, THERE.

OH, I'M SORRY! I DIDN'T REALIZE YOU WERE THERE!
THAT'S ALL RIGHT.
IT'S MY FAULT FOR STANDING BY THE DOOR.
SEEMS I'VE COME AT A BUSY TIME...

BUT LOOK! THIS IS *HARRIAN* LACE!

I THINK IT'S NICE. MAKES YOU LOOK PROPER. INTELLIGENT, EVEN!

WOOD SORREL EMBROIDERY? IS THAT *STILL* IN FASHION?

THE CASTLE MARKETS RAN OUT OF THIS AGES AGO!

EXCUSE ME, BUT DO YOU HAVE ANY MORE LACE LIKE THIS?
WE DO! JUST ONE MOMENT.

COCO!
HOW ABOUT A HAND?

AND YOU, SIR? WHAT CAN WE HELP YOU WITH?
I NEED A LENGTH OF SMOKE-COLORED CLOTH, BUT...
I CAN COME BACK IF YOU'RE BUSY.
I've got the measurements right here.

I CAN CUT THAT FOR YOU.
YOU?

COCO KNOWS HER STUFF.
IS THAT SO?

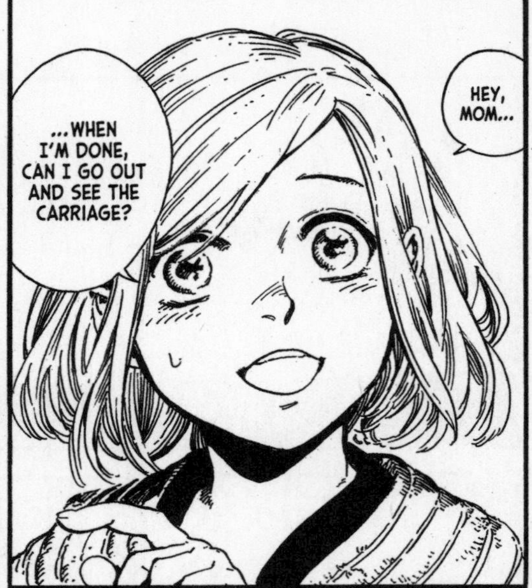
HEY, MOM...
...WHEN I'M DONE, CAN I GO OUT AND SEE THE CARRIAGE?

WHAT HAVE I TOLD YOU ABOUT PLAYING WITH OTHER PEOPLE'S PROPERTY?
YOU BREAK THAT THING, THERE'S NO WITCH AROUND TO FIX IT, Y'KNOW.
I WON'T TOUCH! I'M JUST GONNA LOOK!

PLEASE? I PROMISE TO STOP TALKING ABOUT...
...HOW I WISH I COULD USE MAGIC.

OH, HEAVENS ...

FINE. BUT ONLY IF YOU'RE QUICK ABOUT FINISHING YOUR WORK!
HOORAY!

...
Gotta hurry. Gotta hurry.
Go, go, go!

バ
FWISH
サッ

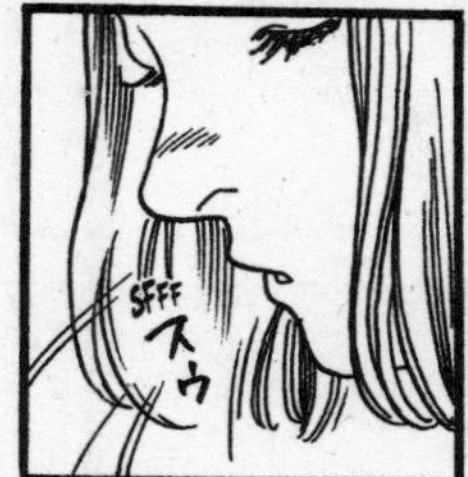
SFFF
スゥ

TICK
ピッ
TICK
ピッ

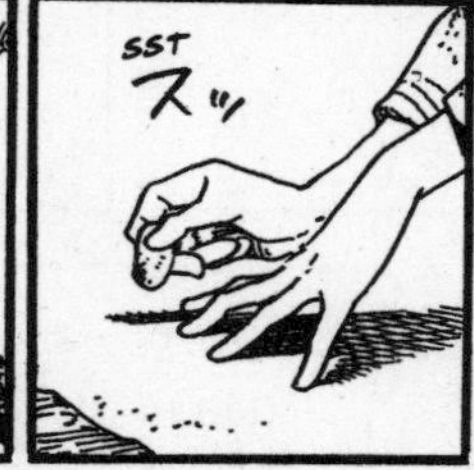
SST
スッ

シャッ
SHICK

ピー
SSSSSSSST

FFFS
フーッ

!

QUITE THE CONCEN-TRATION.
STEADY HANDS, TOO.

MY, MY...
じ
STAAAARE
Eeep! H-Has he been watching this whole time?!
D...
Does he have to stand so close?!

THIS IS SOME *REAL* MAGIC.

PRECISE MEASURE-MENT... A PERFECTLY STRAIGHT CUT...
I HAD NO IDEA THIS VILLAGE WAS HOME TO SUCH AN ARTISAN.

MAGIC'S ALL...
...SPARKLY, AND MYSTERIOUS...
PUMP
...AND WONDERFUL, AND PRICE-LESS...
...AND... AND...
PUMP
PUMP
PUMP

WHOA, WHOA, WHOA! YOU'VE GOT IT ALL WRONG!
NOT TRUE!
NO WAY!
UH-UH!

... BEAUTI-FUL...
Ohhhhh...
...AND...
...PRE-CIOUS.

What am I even saying...?
IT... WOULD APPEAR YOU ARE QUITE FOND OF MAGIC.
AHH...

MIGHT I INQUIRE AS TO WHY?

WHEN I WAS REALLY LITTLE, MY MOM ONCE TOOK ME TO A FESTIVAL AT THE CASTLE...
I BOUGHT A SLIM BOOK THAT DAY...
...FROM A WITCH WEARING A MASK.
A SLIM BOOK?
MM-HM!
Seemed like it was handmade.

YOU THERE, GIRL. WOULDN'T YOU...
...LIKE TO BUY A PICTURE BOOK ABOUT MAGIC?
"MAGIC"?
I LIKE PICTURE BOOKS.
BUT... WHAT'S "MAGIC"?
MAGIC, MY DEAR...
...IS THE MIRACLE THAT MAKES OUR WORLD VIBRANT...

PEGASUS CARRIAGES THAT SOAR ACROSS THE SKY...
SPRINGS OF PURE WATER THAT LAST FOR ALL ETERNITY...
EVEN THE COBBLESTONES AT YOUR FEET, GENTLY GLOWING AS YOU STRIDE ALONG...
ALL THESE THINGS ARE THANKS TO MAGIC.
WOW! IT'S SO PRETTY ...!
MAGIC IS THE BESTEST ...!
I LOVE MAGIC!
INDEED. SO, HOW ABOUT IT? I'LL THROW IN THIS FREE WAND.

AND SO THIS WITCH TALKED YOU INTO BUYING IT, HUH?
I GAVE YOU THAT MONEY BECAUSE YOU TOLD ME YOU WANTED A ROASTED STRAWBERRY TREAT, YOU KNOW.
BUT IT'S SO AMAZING!
A PICTURE BOOK ABOUT MAGIC!
RUMMAGE
RUMMAGE
RUMMAGE
RUMMAGE
AND, UM...
AND THE MAGIC PERSON... EVEN GAVE ME A FREE WAND!
TA-DAH!
SEE? ON THE BOTTOM, IT'S A PEN!
IT CAME WITH INK, TOO!
WHEN I GROW UP...
...I'M GONNA BE A WITCH AND MAKE THE WORLD VIBRANT, TOO!
YOU CAN'T.
SHOCK
HUH?! WHY NOT?!

YOU CAN'T BECOME A WITCH. YOU HAVE TO BE BORN THAT WAY.
REGULAR FOLK LIKE US JUST DON'T HAVE WHAT IT TAKES.
BUT LOOK! WHEN I WALK, THE GROUND LIGHTS UP!
ALL RIGHT. LET'S HEAD ON HOME, AND IF THE GROUND KEEPS GLOWING ALL THE WAY THERE...
...THEN MAYBE YOU CAN USE MAGIC, AFTER ALL.

I MEAN, I THOUGHT WITH ALL THE MONEY I SPENT ON THAT LITTLE BOOK, IT MIGHT SHOW *HOW* TO USE MAGIC, BUT...
...
OHHHHH...

FRET FRET FRET FRET FRET FRET FRET FRET
I COULDN'T STOP HOPING THAT MAYBE...
EVER SINCE THEN, I'VE JUST LIKED WATCHING IT, AND I GUESS...
FRET FRET FRET FRET

A WITCH...
...SELLING BOOKS AT THE CASTLE FESTIVAL?

WHAT'S ALL THAT?
SOMETHING OUTSIDE?
THAT WAS *LOUD*...

IF YOU DON'T MIND, PERHAPS YOU COULD TELL ME MORE AB—
CRASH
Eek!
Whoa!
JOLT
WHIRL

I DON'T BELIEVE THIS!
!

HIS HEAD HIT THE BOTTOM AND IT FELL OVER.
TATTLE-TALE!

WE DIDN'T EVEN TOUCH IT! IT JUST FELL APART!
NUH-UH. TANERL WAS CRAWLING AROUND UNDER-NEATH.

WHAT HAVE YOU DONE TO OUR CARRIAGE?!
THAT BELONGS TO *MY FATHER*, YOU KNOW!
WHAT ARE YOU GOING TO *DO* ABOUT THIS?!

AN APOLOGY WON'T GET US *HOME!*
THESE *BUMPKINS* MUST HAVE PLANNED TO *STRAND* US AND *TAKE* OUR VALU—
DON'T BE ABSURD*!* WE WOULD NEVER...*!*
SEETHE
FUME

I'M TERRIBLY SORRY.
THE CHILDREN'S BEHAVIOR WAS *QUITE* INEXCUS-ABLE.

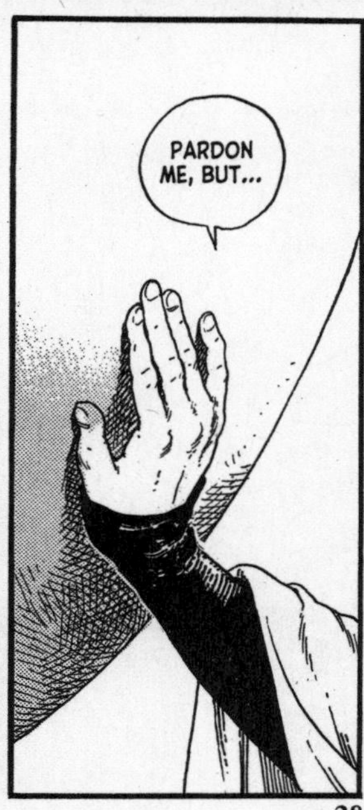
PARDON ME, BUT...

PERHAPS *I* COULD BE OF SERVICE?

QIFREY THE WITCH...

...AT YOUR SERVICE.

COCO!
YOU CAN USE OUR WORKSHOP!

THAT HAT! YOU REALLY *ARE* A WITCH. CAN YOU FIX IT?
I MERELY HAVE TO RE-CAST THE SPELL ON THE CARRIAGE'S BASEBOARD.
OF COURSE, THAT'S A LITTLE DIFFICULT OUTDOORS ...

WE'D BE *DELIGHTED! RIGHT,* MOM?!
HEAVENS, CHILD. YOUR FACE IS BEET RED.
You really want this, don't you?

HE'S A *REAL, LIVE* WITCH!
THIS KIND OF THING *NEVER* HAPPENS AROUND HERE!
FLAP FLAP FLAP FLAP FLAP FLAP
だばだばだばだばだばだば

AND BESIDES...
...WE MIGHT EVEN GET A CHANCE TO *SEE* IT...

THE MOMENT WHEN HE CASTS HIS SPELL!
OH WOW OH WOW OH WOW
I'M SMILING SO HARD, I THINK MY FACE IS GOING TO BREAK! HANG IN THERE, LITTLE SMILE MUSCLES!!
AHH! THIS IS SOOOO AMAZING!
IT'S JUST UN-BE-LIEVABLE!!

ERM, IT'S UH... COCO...
JOLT

...RIGHT?
...UH-HUH?

MANY THANKS.
THE USE OF YOUR WORKSHOP WOULD BE MOST WELCOME.
AND... I WONDER IF I COULD IMPOSE ONE MORE REQUEST.

JUST A LITTLE SOMETHING YOU COULD HELP WITH.
WOULD YOU MIND?

I'D LIKE YOU TO WATCH THE DOOR FOR ME, AND MAKE CERTAIN...
...THERE'S NOBODY PEEKING AS I CAST THE SPELL.
NO ONE IS TO COME INSIDE. NO MATTER WHAT.
GOT THAT?

MY HOPES AND DREAMS, DASHED TO PIECES...
My poor little smile muscles, utterly betrayed...

WHAT'S SO BAD ABOUT WATCHING, ANYWAY?

HEY! WHAT DO YOU THINK YOU'RE DOING?!
UGH! BUSTED!
WHAT? IT'S JUST COCO.

THERE'S MAGIC ALL OVER THE WORLD.
WHY WOULD THE PART WHEN IT GETS CAST BE SUCH A BIG SECRET?
そろーー
SLINK
Ooo

そそくさーー
SHWOOP
Huh?

...IF YOU GET TO LOOK INSIDE...
THEN I DO, TOO!

WE'RE GONNA CHECK OUT THE SKYLIGHT. MAYBE WE CAN SEE INSIDE.
NO! THAT'S NOT FAIR!

WHOA. SHE MADE IT UP.
MOVE OVER!

...

AW, COME ON! THE *CURTAINS* ARE SHUT!
THIS STINKS! LET'S GET OUTTA HERE.

バサァァ
FWOOSH
!!

EEEK!
WH-
WHAT'S
GOING
ON...?!

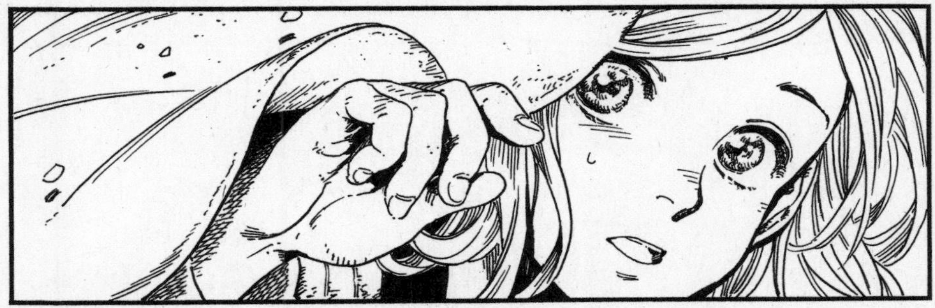

チラ
PEEK

WAIT! I SHOULDN'T!
BUT I...
...REALLY WANT TO SEE...
BUT I'M NOT SUPPOSED TO...

HE'S... DRAWING.

MAGIC BEING CAST...
...WITH A PEN?!

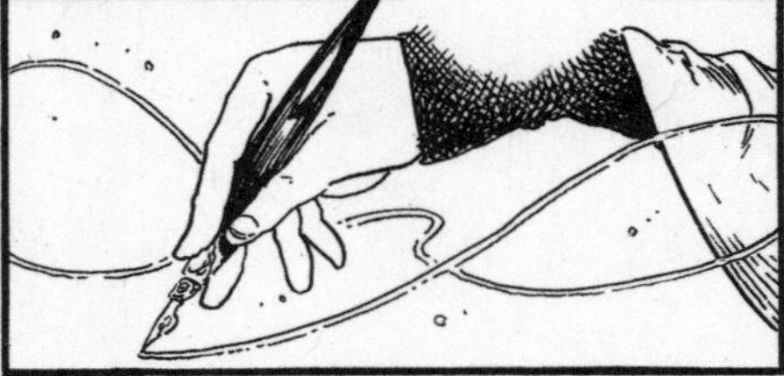

SO THAT'S HOW IT WORKS...

MAGIC ISN'T CAST WITH WORDS...
IT'S DRAWN...!

HM?
RAP
RAP
IT'S DONE, COCO. ...YOU STILL THERE?

NOW THEN...
COCO.
!

ドキッ!!
JOLT

ERM... THANKS FOR THE HARD WORK?
...?

COCO?

WELL, LOOK AT THAT!
IT TOOK OFF!

AREN'T YOU EXCITED? YOU COULDN'T STOP CHATTERING ON ABOUT THAT CARRIAGE EARLIER.
I-I'M OKAY...
HEAVENS, TO THINK A DAY WOULD COME WHEN YOU WEREN'T HOPPING UP AND DOWN ABOUT MAGIC...

HOPPING UP AND DOWN, HM?
JUMP

H- HERE'RE YOUR THINGS! AND THE CLOTH!
OOF!

FWIP

I WOULD HAVE LIKED TO HEAR MORE ABOUT THAT BOOK...
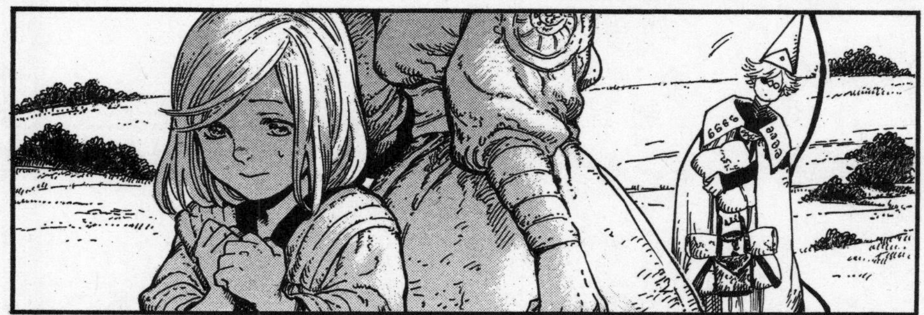

...BUT I SUPPOSE I'LL HAVE NO SUCH LUCK.
I'LL BE ON MY WAY, THEN.
PERHAPS OUR PATHS WILL CROSS AGAIN SOMEDAY.

WERE YOU WORRIED ABOUT SOMETHING?

!
WHEW!

THOUGHT THAT MAYBE...
...YOU WERE GONNA SAY YOU WANTED TO GO WITH THAT MAN.

I'D NEVER DO THAT!
I COULDN'T LEAVE YOU ALL ALONE!

I ALREADY LOST YOUR FATHER TO ILLNESS. I DON'T THINK I COULD BEAR HAVING YOU LEAVE, TOO...

THANKS, COCO. HOW'D I GET SUCH A SWEET GIRL?

I WON'T LEAVE. BUT THERE'S SOMETHING I HAVE TO TRY.

...I'M SORRY, MOM.

ALL THE PATTERNS INSIDE THE PICTURE BOOK...
...AND THE WAND THROWN IN FOR FREE...

THE PEN TIP WAS NO COINCIDENCE.
THE PEN *ITSELF* WAS THE WAND...!

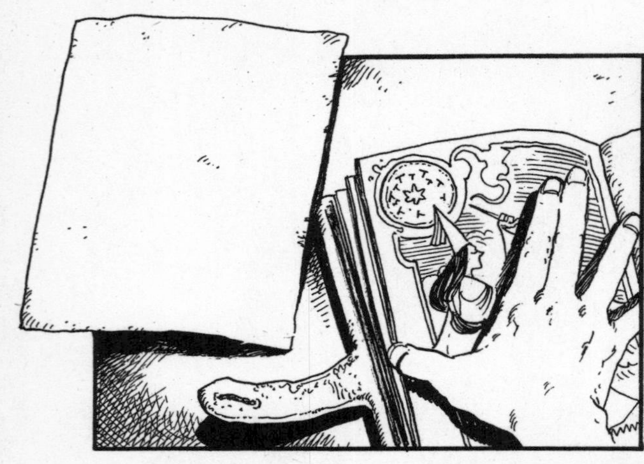

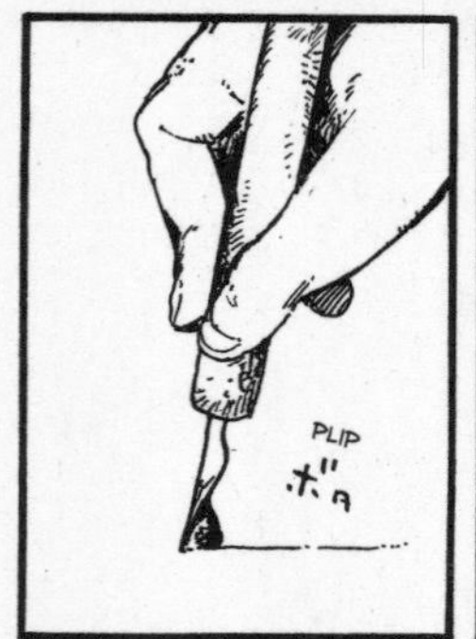
PLIP
ポタ

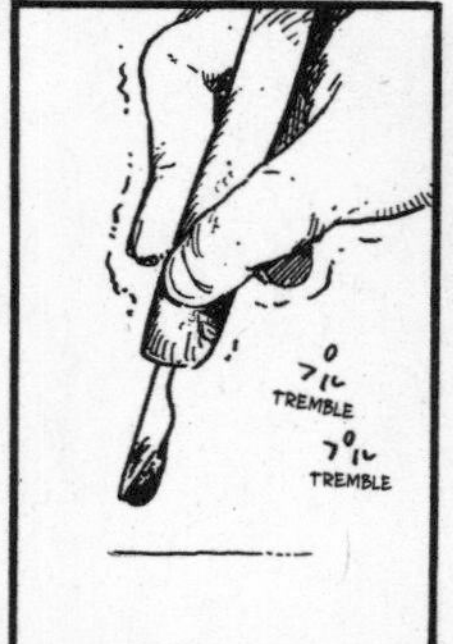
プル
TREMBLE
プル
TREMBLE

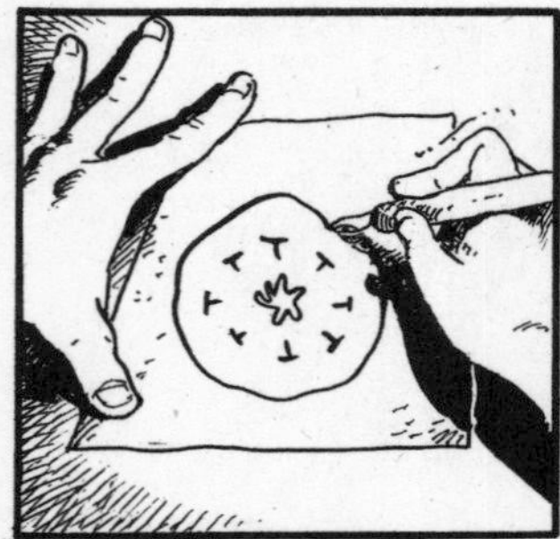

IT'S MAGIC! MAGIC! REAL MAGIC!
OH MY! OH MY!
OH MY!
THIS IS AMAZING! I DON'T EVEN KNOW WHAT TO DO!
THWAP
THWAP
BMFF
OH MY! OH MY! OH MY!
BMFF
DRAWING! THAT'S BEEN THE SECRET THIS WHOLE TIME!

IT GLOWED! JUST NOW! I DON'T BELIEVE IT!
I JUST USED MAGIC!
OH MY!
OH MY!
OH MY!

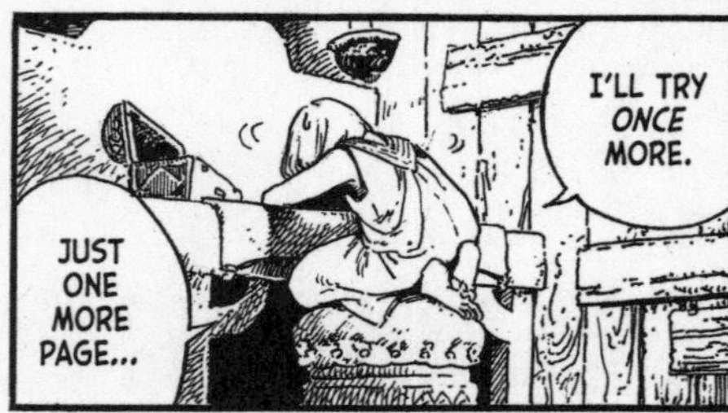
I'LL TRY ONCE MORE.
JUST ONE MORE PAGE...

I WASN'T SUPPOSED TO LOOK, THOUGH. AM I GONNA GET IN TROUBLE IF ANYONE FINDS OUT...?
OOOHHHHH...

A PICTURE BOOK, HM?

I JUST CAN'T GET IT OUT OF MY MIND.

TO SELL SOMETHING...

...PERTAINING TO MAGIC TO A CHILD WHO KNOWS NOTHING OF THE ART...

BWOOF
ボッ

AHHH! THAT ONE WAS A *FIRE* SPELL!!
STOP! STOP! GO OUT, PLEASE!!

PHEWWW...
That could've been bad.

I THINK I'M GETTING THE HANG OF THIS!

BUT...
FLAP
ぱた
FLAP
ぱた

BIG ONES ARE STRONGER THAN LITTLE ONES...

BLEH
...AND NEATLY DRAWN ONES LAST LONGER THAN MESSY ONES!

BUT IT'S HARD TO DRAW THEM BOTH BIG *AND* NEAT.
THE VISITOR WE HAD TODAY MADE IT LOOK SO EASY...

WAIT! THAT'S IT!

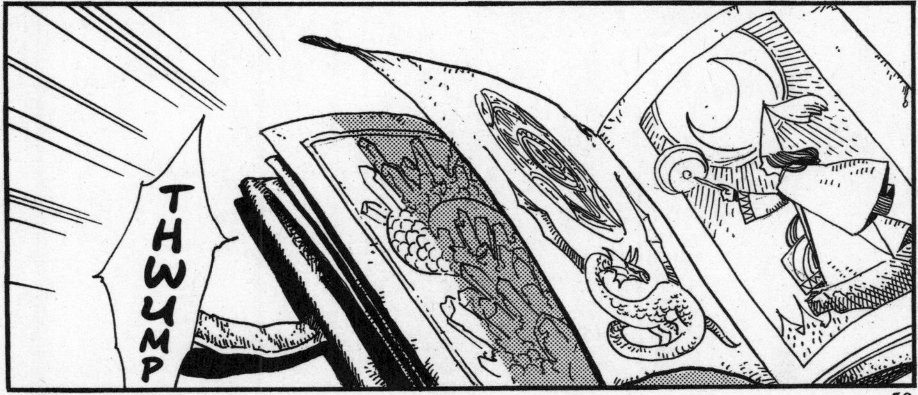
THWUMP

HAH! JUST LIKE I THOUGHT!

IF I PUT THE PAPER ON THE BOOK...

...I CAN SEE THROUGH IT AND TRACE THE PATTERN PERFECTLY!

THERE!
I WONDER WHAT KIND OF SPELL THIS ONE I—

FLASH

SNAP
TMP
TMP
TMP
PWOOF
FWAAAAAH

THRUST

...!
SQUEEZE

WHAT DID YOU DRAW, COCO?!
WHAT KIND OF MAGIC DID YOU DRAW?!!

I... I DON'T KNOW!
I JUST TRACED ONE OF THE PATTERNS IN THE BOOK AND...!

COCO?

THE BOOK!
IS IT STILL INSIDE?
Y...
YEAH!

WAIT! THAT'S...

MOM!
HOLD STILL!
I DON'T WANT TO DROP YOU!

KRKK

COCO!!

KRRKKKK
?!
KRRKKKK

NO...
THIS CAN'T BE REAL...

MOMMY!!

I... I'M...
I'M SORRY...
I DIDN'T KNOW WHAT...

OF COURSE YOU DIDN'T.
THAT'S WHY IT'S KEPT SECRET. TO PREVENT THINGS LIKE *THIS*.

THE CONJURING INK... THE PATTERNS ...
FOR THE CASTING SEALS...
THAT'S ALL IT TAKES. WITH THOSE, *ANYONE* CAN USE MAGIC.
HIDING THAT TRUTH IS THE ***ONE GREAT RULE OF WITCHES.***

AND THOSE WHO FIND OUT...
...MUST HAVE THEIR MEMORIES ERASED.

I CAN'T HOLD ON TO YOU LIKE THIS!
C-CALM DOWN...!
QUIT TWISTING AROUND!
NOOO! LET GO! LET GO OF ME!
SHAKE
SHAKE
SHAKE
SHAKE
SHAKE
SHAKE
SHAKE

KICK
BFF!

AHHHH!
IF YOU MAKE ME FORGET...
...THEN WHAT'LL HAPPEN TO MY MOM?!
AHHHH!

IF YOU COULD TELL ME WHAT KIND OF SEAL YOU DREW, I MIGHT KNOW HOW TO REVERSE IT, BUT...
IF YOU'RE ASKING ABOUT THE PICTURE BOOK, I'VE READ IT SO MANY TIMES, I KNOW IT BY HEART!
KICK
KICK
KICK
...WITHOUT THAT KNOWLEDGE... OWWW!
AHHHHH!
AHHH!
WOBBLE

OF COURSE! THE *BOOK*!

IF THAT BOOK WAS WRITTEN BY THOSE WHOM I SUSPECT...
...I CANNOT ALLOW HER TO FORGET.
SHE'S THE ONLY LEAD I HAVE.

GRRRPHHH!
NNGGHHH!
YOU COULD IDENTIFY THE BOOK IF YOU SAW IT AGAIN, YES?
COULD YOU POINT OUT WHICH PAGE YOU DREW FROM?

GASP!
IF I FOUND ANOTHER COPY FOR YOU...
...AND SHOWED YOU THE SHAPE...

THE SAME ONE I DREW...
IF YOU SAW IT, COULD YOU SAVE MY MOTHER?

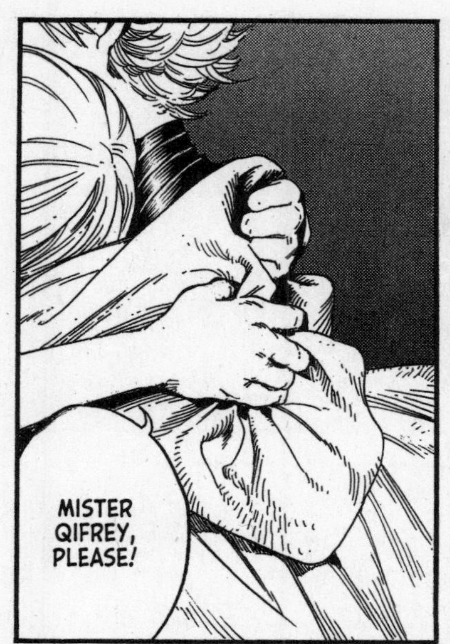

PLEASE DON'T TAKE MY MEMORIES!

I SWEAR I'LL FIND THE BOOK AGAIN!

I'LL DO *ANYTHING!*

ANYTHING TO SAVE HER!!

THAT IS YOUR ONLY OPTION.

...FROM NOW ON...
...YOU WILL BE...
COCO...
...A WITCH.
CHAPTER 1 ♦ END

Witch Hat Atelier

FWISH
I HEAR WIND...
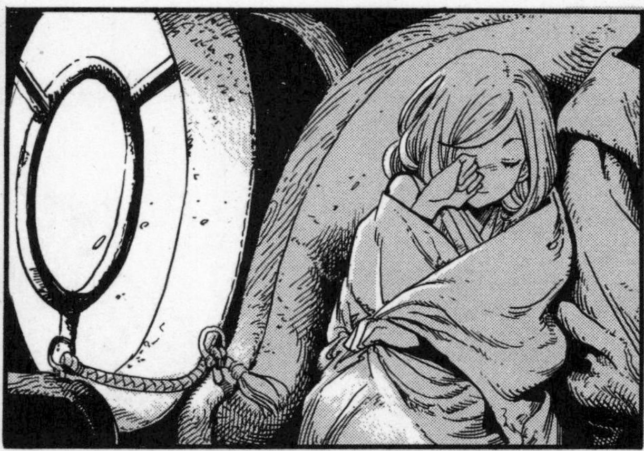
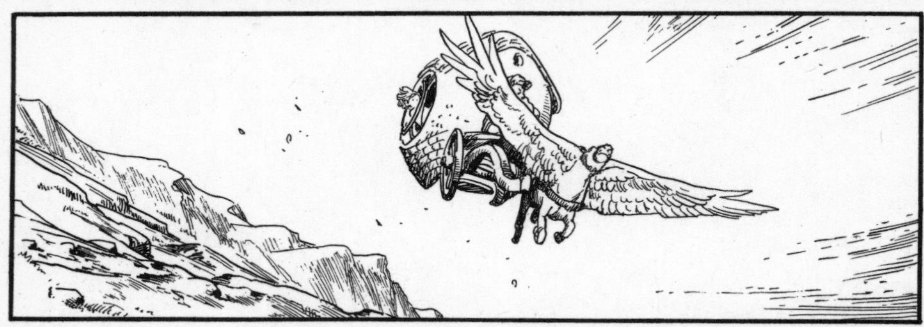

MUST BE A BIT CHILLY UP HERE IN JUST YOUR BEDCLOTHES.
DON'T WORRY. WE'LL BE ARRIVING SOON.

AH, YOU'RE UP. I HAILED US A PASSING CARRIAGE.

SEE? THERE IT IS.

MY ATELIER.
AND YOUR NEW PLACE OF STUDY.
CHAPTER 2

I'VE STREWN GUARD BRIAR SEEDS AROUND YOUR HOME.
THE BRANCHES WILL GROW QUICKLY INTO A FORMIDABLE BARRIER.
I THOUGHT IT WISE TO STAVE OFF ANY CARELESS VISITORS UNTIL WE DISCOVER THE NATURE OF THAT SPELL.
I'M AFRAID IT WILL BE SOME TIME...
...BEFORE YOU SEE HOME AGAIN, AND...
COCO?

WHAT'S THE TROUBLE?

I PROMISED HER...

I PROMISED THAT I'D NEVER LEAVE HER ON HER OWN.
THAT I'D NEVER ABANDON HER.
I...

COCO...

PLEASE DON'T BLAME YOURSELF.
YOU HAD NO WAY TO KNOW.

HERE. RINSE YOUR FACE.

LET OUT ALL THOSE TEARS AND EMBRACE THE FUTURE!

STARTING TODAY, THIS IS YOUR NEW HOME.

BLUB

UM...
WHAT IS THIS STUFF?
WATER, OF COURSE.
?

Umm... I don't remember water being this round and... Floaty.
AH!
HOW COULD I FORGET?!

WHAT'S THERE TO BE SCARED OF?!

'CAUSE TOUCHING MAGIC I'VE NEVER SEEN BEFORE...

...KINDA GIVES ME THE *CREEPS* NOW.

IT'S NOT LIKE THERE'S ANYTHING TRICKY ABOUT THAT SPELL.
I'M TETIA. WANT ME TO SHOW YOU HOW THAT THING WORKS?
IT'S CALLED A VAPOR BUBBLE.
IT'S A SPELL THAT COLLECTS MOISTURE FROM THE AIR INTO WATER WE CAN USE!
HOP
IF YOU TIP THE LOWER TRAY, WATER POURS RIGHT OUT! SEE?
GLUP GLUP GLUP

THANK YOU!
HUH?

WOW! THAT'S INCREDIBLE!
THANK YOU!

I LOVE IT WHEN PEOPLE TELL ME "THANK YOU"!
SO THANK YOU FOR YOUR THANKS!

JUST IGNORE HER...

OH... UH... I SEE. TH-THANKS...
AND THANK YOU AGAIN FOR THANKING ME!
THIS ISN'T EVER GOING TO STOP, IS IT...?
PUMP

HOW COULD YOU SAY THAT, RICHEH?
I WAS JUST HELPING OUT!
"Just leave her be"...?

WHEN TETIA GETS EXCITED, JUST LEAVE HER BE.
IF YOU STOP RESPONDING, EVENTUALLY SHE QUIETS DOWN.

...HUH?

SHE'S HOLDING A PEN. AND INK.
ARE THEY FOR CASTING MAGIC...?

ARE YOU BOTH WITCHES?
APPREN-TICES, MORE PRECISELY.
WE'RE STUDENTS OF MASTER QIFREY!

WAIT. DOES THAT MEAN YOU'RE *NOT?*
HUH?
HUH?
WAIT.
HUH?
I WAS POSITIVE YOU WERE HERE TO STUDY, JUST LIKE US.
HUH?
WHAT?
HUH?
HUH?
YOU LOOK LIKE YOU'RE OUR AGE.
HUH?
SO...
UM...
WHICH ATELIER DO YOU BELONG TO?

OH, WELL, I'M NOT EXACTLY AN APPRENTICE YET...
I MEAN, I ONLY DREW MY FIRST SPELL YESTERDAY...
THIS IS MY NEW HOME, STARTING TODAY.

HUH?

UM...

THE OUTSIDER WHO DREW FORBIDDEN SPELLS.

THE ONE ALLOWED TO BECOME AN APPRENTICE, MEMORY INTACT.

ARE YOU ALL RIGHT?
OH, MISTER QIFREY...

JOLT
HERE YOU ARE, COCO.

AGOTT'S AWAY, I SEE...
TETIA, RICHEH? COULD YOU LET COCO AND ME SPEAK IN PRIVATE?
OKAY!

DON'T BE AFRAID.
I'LL EXPLAIN EVERY-THING.

LONG AGO, MAGIC WAS JUST ANOTHER ORDINARY PART OF LIFE.

ANYONE, FROM ANY PLACE, COULD CAST...
ALL IT TOOK WAS KNOWLEDGE OF PRESCRIBED DESIGNS...
...AND SPECIALLY CRAFTED INK.
...AND MAGIC WAS FAMILIAR TO ALL.
HOWEVER, BECAUSE OF THAT...
...THE WORLD WAS CONSTANTLY EMBROILED IN WAR.

MANY FOUL SPELLS WERE CONCEIVED...
FOR WHEN MAN HAS THE POWER TO DO ANYTHING, THEN ANYTHING HE WILL DO.
...PROMPTING THE FEW GOOD SOULS LEFT IN THE WORLD TO RENOUNCE WAR AND BAND TOGETHER AS THE KEEPERS OF MAGIC.
...AND PASSED ON KNOWLEDGE OF THE ART ONLY TO APPRENTICES WHO COULD BE TRUSTED TO GUARD THE SECRET.
THEY ERASED THE MEMORIES OF MAGIC FROM THE POPULACE...

SINCE THE DAY OF THE PACT, WE HAVE SPREAD THE BELIEF...
...THAT MAGIC CAN ONLY BE WIELDED BY THOSE WITH INNATE POWER.
IF THE TRUTH WERE TO PROLIFERATE ONCE MORE...
...OUR WORLD WOULD BE THRUST INTO CHAOS ANEW.

THAT IS WHY WE ARE CAUTIOUS TO KEEP IT HIDDEN.
AND THAT IS WHY YOUR CASE SPARKS SUCH GOSSIP.
...I'M SORRY FOR THAT, COCO.

NO. IT'S MY OWN FAULT.

BUT... THERE'S ONE OTHER THING...
ギュ
CLENCH
THE FORBIDDEN SPELLS. WHAT ARE THEY...?

...SPELLS DRAWN DURING THAT AGE OF WAR, SHUT AWAY FROM THE WORLD ON THE DAY OF THE PACT.

THEY ARE SPELLS MEANT TO HURT PEOPLE.

CLATTER
カタン
SHOW THEM TO ME!
LET ME SEE ALL THE SPELLS THAT...
...MUST NOT BE USED!
I WANT TO KNOW THEM!

I CAN'T GO ON, NOT KNOWING...
...WHAT THEY ARE.
IT'S TOO FRIGHTENING TO BEAR.

NORMALLY, I'D COUNSEL PATIENCE. BUT THAT'S NOT SO EASY IN YOUR CASE.

COME. LET ME SHOW YOU SOMETHING.

THE FORBIDDEN SPELLS ARE TOO NUMEROUS TO COUNT.
BUT THEY CAN BE SUMMED UP RATHER SIMPLY.
MAGIC THAT DIRECTLY AFFECTS THE HUMAN BODY OR MIND...
...IS NOT TO BE CAST AT ANY TIME.

TRANSFORMATIONS, SPELLS OF AGING OR DE-AGING...
...TELEPORTATION WITHOUT THE USE OF DOORS OR VEHICLES...
...SPELLS TO CONTROL OTHERS' MINDS OR EMOTIONS...
...OR THOSE TO HARM OR EVEN HEAL THE BODY. ALL SUCH SPELLS.

WITH ONE EXCEPTION.

THE SPELL TO MAKE PEOPLE FORGET...?

PRECISELY.

WOW...

THINGS LIKE...
...CAR-RIAGES AND LAMPS.

THUS, MOST MAGIC IS USED TO CREATE MAGICAL TOOLS.
SKETCH
SKETCH

OR WINDOWS ...

...SUCH AS THIS.

WHEN WE ARRIVED HERE, THERE WAS NOTHING BUT HILLS...

THERE'S A LAKE!

DO YOU SEE THE STRUCTURE IN THE DISTANCE?
IT'S A WINDOW-WAY.
IT CONNECTS TO ITS ANALOGUES, OTHER WINDOWS OF THE SAME DESIGN.

THAT IS THE TOWER OF TOMES. A VAULT OF KNOWLEDGE.

THE MOMENT ANY BOOK ON MAGIC IS COMPOSED, IT IS INSTANTLY REPLICATED WITHIN THAT TOWER.

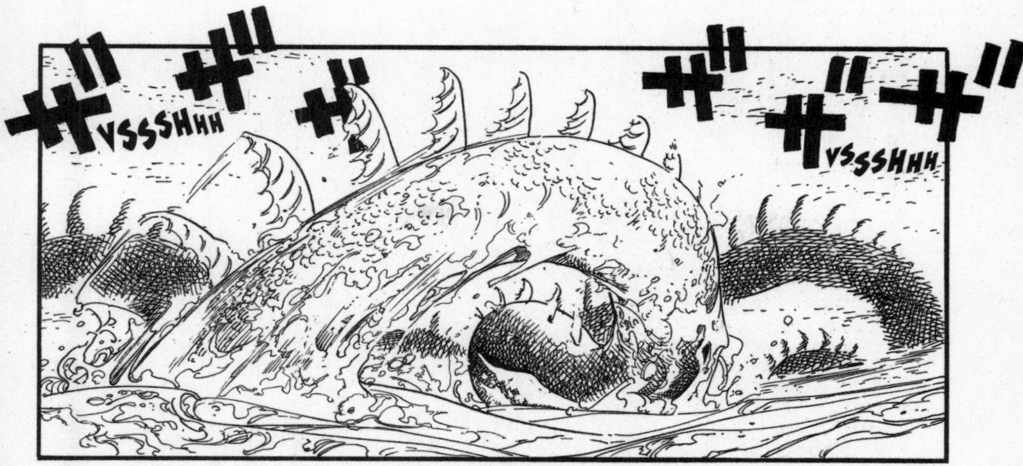
VSSSHHH
VSSSHHH

FERSPLSHH

GRRRKK

FOR *THAT*, YOU SEE, IS THE LIBRARIANS' TRIAL.

?!

THE TOWER OF TOMES IS PROTECTED BY FOUR LIBRARIANS.
ONLY WITCHES WHO OVERCOME THE TRIAL ARE PERMITTED INSIDE.

IN ORDER TO ENTER THE TOWER, FIRST YOU WILL HAVE TO STUDY.

COCO...
I WAS QUITE DELIGHTED TO HEAR...
...OF YOUR THIRST FOR KNOWLEDGE.
IT'S ONLY NATURAL TO FEEL AFRAID.
BUT...

GRRRKK
KNOW THAT THOSE SPELLS WHICH ARE NOT FORBIDDEN...
...ARE ALL MEANS TO BRING HAPPINESS TO PEOPLE.

IF YOU'RE GOING TO LEARN...
...THEN WHY NOT KNOW MORE ABOUT THE SPELLS OF KINDNESS?
JUST A THOUGHT.
BUT PERHAPS YOU AGREE?
...I'D LIKE THAT...
...MASTER QIFREY!

FWOOSH

GOOD TO HEAR!
WELL, THEN, LET'S SHOW YOU YOUR NEW QUARTERS.

THOUGH I SUPPOSE WE OUGHT TO TIDY *THIS* UP FIRST.

WELCOME TO YOUR NEW ROOM.

IT LOOKS AS THOUGH AGOTT IS STILL AWAY.
WHO'S AGOTT?

YOUR ROOM-MATE.

WORKSPACES ARE SHARED, TWO TO A ROOM.
BEDROOMS ARE SEPARATE, DOWN THE STAIRS IN BACK.
DON'T WORRY, THE BEDROOM DOORS LOCK.

NOW, WHY NOT TAKE A MOMENT TO REST UP?
I HAVE SOME BUSINESS TO ATTEND TO. CALL IF YOU NEED ANYTHING.

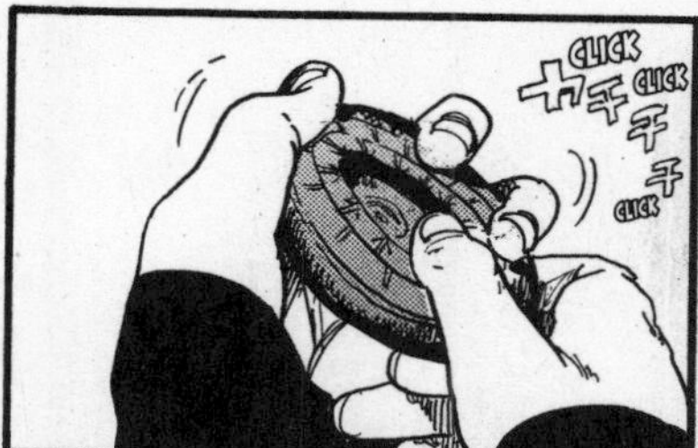
CLICK
CLICK
CLICK

THIS IS QIFREY.

FWIP

ゴン
RUMMAGE

YOUR APPROVAL OF THE GIRL'S APPRENTICESHIP IS DEEPLY APPRECIATED.

NO.
NO PROGRESS YET ON THE BOOK.
SHE'S STILL DISORIENTED, BUT...
...THINGS APPEAR QUITE PROMISING.

WE SHOULD BE QUITE PLEASED BY HER EXCITEMENT FOR MAGIC.
INDEED.
IT WOULD BE AN OBSTACLE WERE SHE TO RECOIL.

FOR THE TIME WILL COME...
...WHEN WE MUST HAVE HER FACE THE FORBIDDEN SPELLS.

SO THIS IS HOW...
...A WITCH'S ROOM LOOKS.

THAT SIDE IS MINE.

GET OUT OF THE WAY...
...SO I CAN LAND.

TMP
OH! SORRY!

YOU MUST BE AGOTT, RIGHT?
I'M COCO...
I KNOW.

I UNDERSTAND YOU'RE A NEW APPRENTICE HERE.
THE OUTSIDER EVERYONE'S ON ABOUT.

SUCH A SHAME ABOUT YOUR MOTHER.
!

TH... THAN—
THANKS TO *YOU*...

...SHE'LL NEVER BE FLESH AND BLOOD AGAIN.

...!

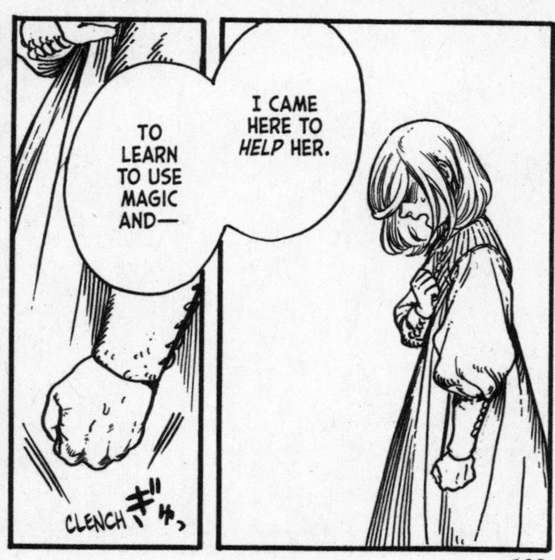
I CAME HERE TO *HELP* HER.
TO LEARN TO USE MAGIC AND—
CLENCH ぎゅっ

THRUST
YOU KNOW NOTHING.

I'VE BEEN PRACTICING THE SEALS EVER SINCE I COULD WRITE. I WEAR THESE STAINS WITH PRIDE.
I PASSED THE TEST TO BECOME A STUDENT OF MAGIC...
...AND WAITED TO BE CHOSEN FOR AN APPRENTICE-SHIP.
AN IGNORANT OUTSIDER LIKE YOU...
...SIMPLY DOESN'T HAVE WHAT IT TAKES.
BUT I...
I'VE ALREADY MANAGED TO DRAW IT ONCE!
I AT LEAST HAVE TO TRY!
THEN...
...PROVE YOURSELF.

Chapter 2 ♦ End

Witch Hat
Atelier

Chapter 3

コォォォ…
KHOOO

IT...
IT JUST DISAPPEARED INTO THE VOID...
KNOCK KNOCK
COCO?
YOU DONE IN THERE YET?
SORRY. JUST FINISHED.

GOOD MORNING.
MORN-ING...
COCO.

HEY, TETIA...
ARE ALL MAGICAL WASHROOMS LIKE THAT?

THERE WAS A MAGIC SPRING NEAR MY VILLAGE, BUT...
...NOBODY'S HOUSE HAD ANYTHING LIKE *THAT.*

YEAH, I GUESS MOST CONTRAPTIONS ARE FOUND IN BIG CITIES...

CON...
TRAP-TIONS?

COULD YOU TELL ME MORE ABOUT WHAT KIND OF STUFF THERE IS?
UM... SORRY. I'M KINDA BUSY...
BUT I'VE GOT A BOOK YOU CAN BORROW!

...OKAY.
PWFF

"TOOLS ENCHANTED WITH MAGIC..."
"...ARE KNOWN AS CONTRAPTIONS."

SUCH ITEMS ARE PRIZED THROUGHOUT THE WORLD, AS THEY CAN BE USED EVEN BY THOSE WHO DO NOT PRACTICE MAGIC.
THEY CAN ONLY BE CREATED BY WITCHES AND THEREFORE COMMAND HIGH PRICES.

"THE CRAFTING OF CONTRAPTIONS BEFORE ONE HAS TAKEN THE TEST AND BECOME AN APPRENTICE IS FORBIDDEN."
THE... TEST?
IS THIS WHAT AGOTT WAS TALKING ABOUT?
SHE SAID THERE'S A TEST BEFORE YOU CAN BECOME AN APPRENTICE...

DETAILS ABOUT HOW WHAT'S TAKEN?
EEEP!
SLAM

BUT IT DOESN'T GIVE ANY DETAILS ABOUT *HOW* IT'S TAKEN...

WHAT ARE THESE ...?

THERE ARE MANY ASPECTS OF MAGIC NOT RECORDED IN BOOKS.
THE BEST WAY TO STUDY IS NOT BY READING BUT BY *DOING!*

THEY'RE YOUR COMPO-NENTS...
...AND TOOLS FOR CASTING.

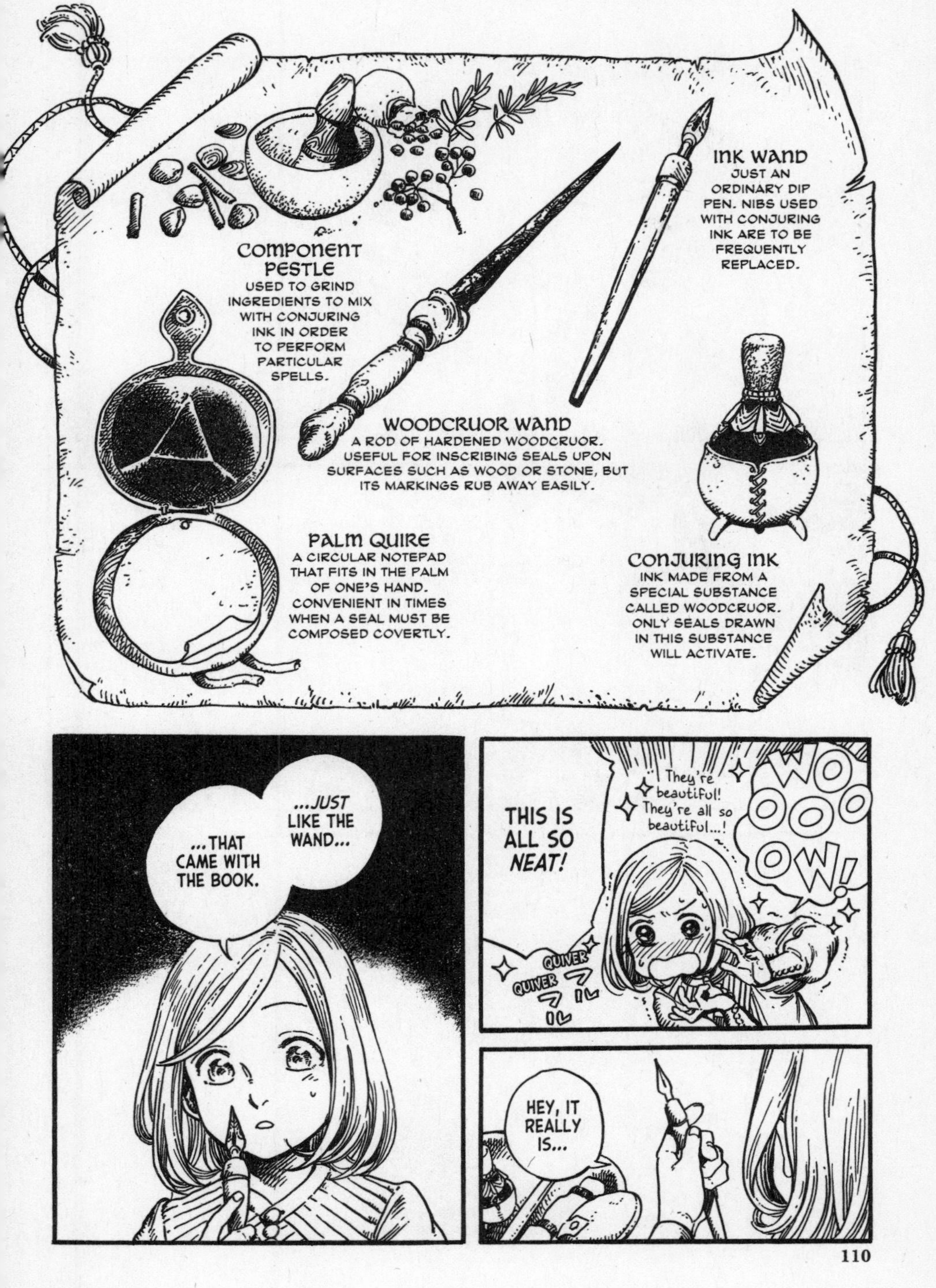

INK WAND
JUST AN ORDINARY DIP PEN. NIBS USED WITH CONJURING INK ARE TO BE FREQUENTLY REPLACED.

COMPONENT PESTLE
USED TO GRIND INGREDIENTS TO MIX WITH CONJURING INK IN ORDER TO PERFORM PARTICULAR SPELLS.

WOODCRUOR WAND
A ROD OF HARDENED WOODCRUOR. USEFUL FOR INSCRIBING SEALS UPON SURFACES SUCH AS WOOD OR STONE, BUT ITS MARKINGS RUB AWAY EASILY.

PALM QUIRE
A CIRCULAR NOTEPAD THAT FITS IN THE PALM OF ONE'S HAND. CONVENIENT IN TIMES WHEN A SEAL MUST BE COMPOSED COVERTLY.

CONJURING INK
INK MADE FROM A SPECIAL SUBSTANCE CALLED WOODCRUOR. ONLY SEALS DRAWN IN THIS SUBSTANCE WILL ACTIVATE.

IT'S AS IF THAT WITCH I MET AT THE FESTIVAL...
...WANTED ME TO USE THE FORBIDDEN SPELLS...

I STILL FEEL KIND OF UNEASY ABOUT IT ALL...
BUT...

I HAVE TO GET MOM BACK TO NORMAL!

WELL, THEN...
COCO...
...SHALL WE BEGIN?

Y...
YES, PLEASE!

HALF A CLOCK MARK LATER
ち SLUMP ん...

First, one fashions the Sigils and Signs on the Contraption, using Woodcruor sourced from the Silverwood Grove of Zozah, and then...
UMMM...?
I WAS ABOUT TO DROWN...
...IN A SEA OF NEW WORDS...
IT JUST FELT LIKE...

ARE YOU ALL RIGHT, COCO?
SHALL WE TAKE A BREAK?
WOBBLE
WOBBLE
I...I'M FINE.

AH, FORGIVE ME... I'VE NEVER GIVEN LESSONS TO A CHILD WHO HASN'T LEARNED THE FUNDAMENTALS...

LET'S TRY THIS. COULD YOU REPEAT BACK TO ME THE THINGS YOU'VE UNDERSTOOD SO FAR?
COCO?
YES!!

O-OKAY...
UM...
SPELLS ARE COMPOSED OF THREE ELEMENTS...

A "SIGIL" IN THE CENTER...
...SURROUNDED BY MARKINGS CALLED "SIGNS"...
What else...
Um...
AND, UH...
...AND AN OUTER "RING" THAT COMPLETES THE SEAL.

Sigil of Light
Sigil of Fire
THERE ARE DIFFERENT TYPES OF SIGILS, LIKE FOR FIRE, WATER, LIGHT, AND WIND... AND THAT DETERMINES THE TYPE OF SPELL...
Sigil of Wind
Sigil of Water
THE SIGNS DETERMINE WHAT FORM THE SPELL WILL TAKE, AS WELL AS ITS SIZE AND DIRECTION.
Sign of Levitation
Sign of Columns
Sign of Dispersion
THAT TOOK EVERYTHING I HAD...
BUT YOU DID A MARVELOUS JOB!
TEETER
TOTTER
AND ONCE THE OUTER RING IS COMPLETED, THE SEAL IS FIXED...
...AND THE SPELL ACTIVATES!

...TO FEATS SUCH AS THIS.

...

FIDGET
FIDGET
SCRIBBLE
SCRIBBLE
SCRIBBLE

?!
CRUMPLE

I...
I WANNA TRY, TOO!
SPLENDID! THAT'S THE SPIRIT!!
HMF
HMF

I CAN'T SHOW YOU MINE RIGHT AFTER YOU SHARED THAT GORGEOUS FLOWER MADE OF WATER!
IT'S SO BAD, AND...
...THE LINES ARE ALL WOBBLY AND JUMBLY, AND...

SNATCH
NO! DON'T THROW IT AWAY!
No! No!
You can't look at that!
NOOO!
GIVE IT BACK!!

THE SPELL CAN'T ACTI-VATE UNTIL THE RING IS WHOLE.
LOOK HERE. THE RING'S NOT CONNECTED.

OF COURSE THEY ARE. YOU'RE STILL LEARNING.

AND IT LOOKS LIKE WE STILL HAVE SOME MORE BASIC ISSUES.

EVERYONE'S UNSTEADY WHEN FIRST USING A NEW TOOL.
JUST AS A NEWBORN FOAL FALTERS AS IT LEARNS TO STAND.
SOON YOU'LL BE FULL OF CONFIDENCE, BOUNDING AS YOU PLEASE.

NOW, LET'S JOIN THOSE ENDS...
...AND SEE WHAT MAGIC RESUL—
PSHAHH
ぷしゃあ!!

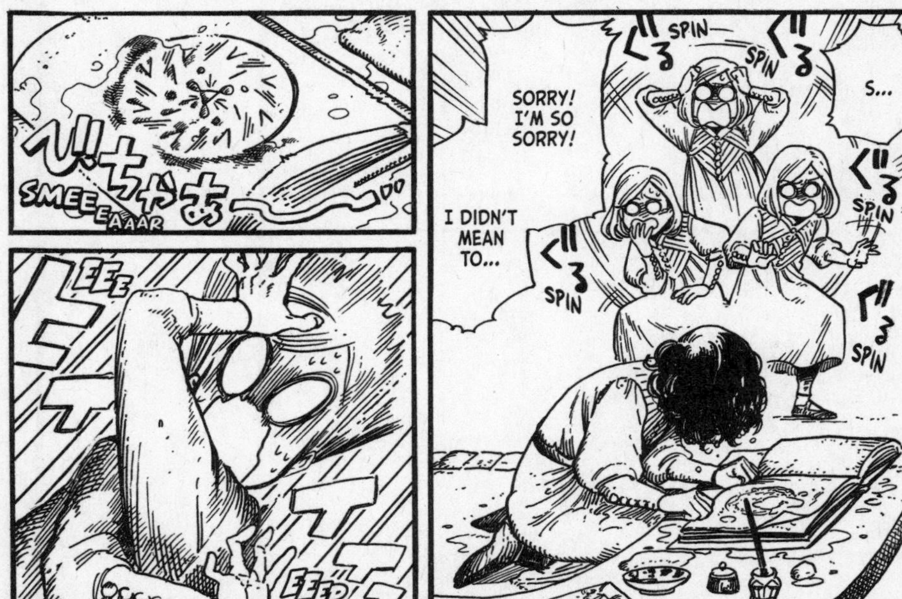
ぴちゃ
SMEEEAAAR
EEEE
EEEP
ぐる SPIN
ぐる SPIN
S...
SORRY! I'M SO SORRY!
I DIDN'T MEAN TO...
ぐる SPIN
ぐる SPIN
ぐる SPIN

I'm so sorry!
FWAP ばふんこ
FWAP ばふんこ
FWAP ばふんこ
HERE! I'LL DRY IT OFF, OKAY?!!
CALM DOWN, COCO!
WE'RE SORRY, AGOTT... ARE YOU ALL RIGHT?
ポタ DRIP
ポタ DRIP

IT'S FINE, MASTER...
IT DOESN'T BOTHER ME.

PERHAPS I COULD TAKE A LOOK AT COCO'S SEAL?
TMP ツカ
ツカ TMP
ツカ TMP
OH... SURE.

AH... HERE'S THE PROBLEM.
LOOK.

THIS ONE SIGN IS LONGER THAN THE REST.
IT'S APPLYING TOO MUCH PRESSURE, CAUSING THE WATER TO SPURT OUT TO THE SIDE.
ASTUTE AS ALWAYS!
YOUR OBSERVATIONS ARE SPOT ON, AGOTT.
Here's a towel for you.
YES...
I THINK COCO WILL DO QUITE WELL IN YOUR HANDS.

AGOTT, PLEASE LOOK AFTER COCO WHILE I'M GONE.
I'LL BE AWAY FOR TWO OR THREE DAYS VISITING THE GREAT HALL.

HUH?!

B-BUT MASTER ...

WAIT! HOLD ON, PLEASE! I DON'T—
TMP TMP
THERE IS MUCH YOU CAN LEARN FROM YOUR PEERS, COCO.
WATCH THEM CLOSELY. STUDY THEIR TECHNIQUE.

TIPTOE

I THINK IT'S ABOUT TIME FOR YOU TO DELVE INTO MORE *SERIOUS* STUDY.

KRSPLSHH
SPLASH
KRSPLSHH
SPLASH
SPLASH
KRSPLSHH

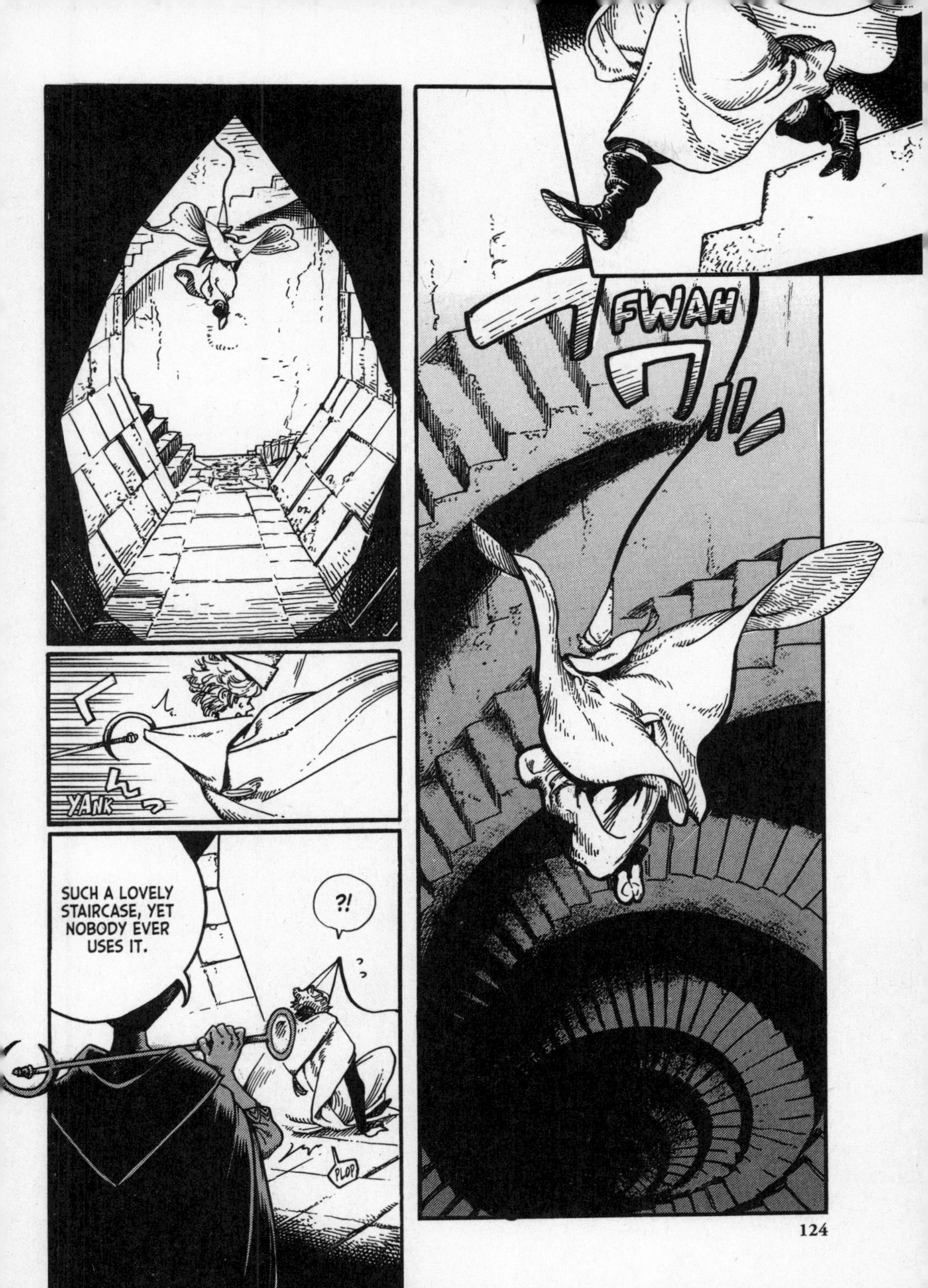

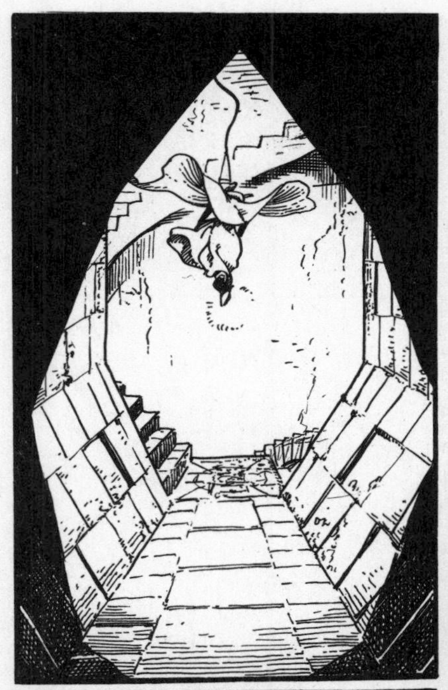

FWAH

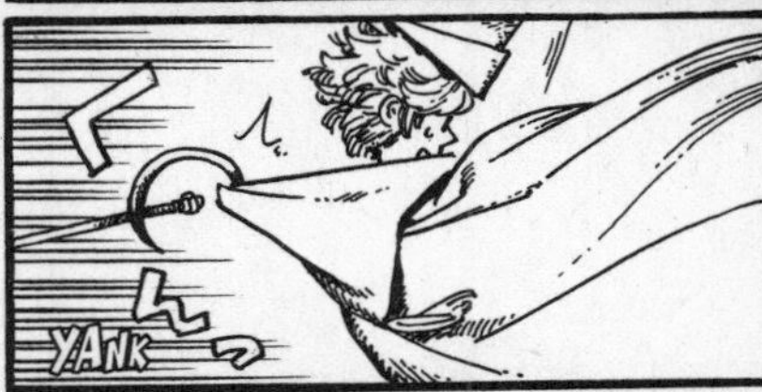

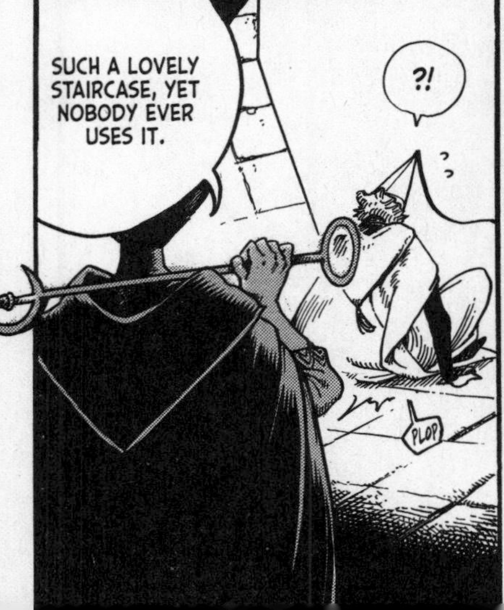

SUCH A LOVELY STAIRCASE, YET NOBODY EVER USES IT.
?!
PLOP

...YOUNG DISSIDENT OF THE GREAT HALL.

IT'S BEEN SOME TIME SINCE YOU LAST SET FOOT ON THE SEABED...

DAYS LONG PAST, ALAIRA.

AND FLEET IT SHOULD BE, IF IT CONCERNS...

WORD IS YOU'VE DONE SOMETHING UNTHINKABLE YET AGAIN.
AND YOU HAVE A NEW APPRENTICE TO SHOW FOR IT!
SO YOU'VE HEARD. NOTHING SO FLEET AS A RUMOR, IS THERE?
ARE THEY...?

...THOSE OF THE BRIMMED CAPS.
!
...
FIRST TIME WE'VE SEEN FORBIDDEN MAGIC IN FOUR YEARS.
SHE'S A LEAD, AND A FIRM ONE... I'D WANT TO KEEP HER CLOSE, TOO.
THAT'S NOT WHY I MADE MY REQUEST.

IT'S TOO SOON FOR HER. AND THE SEASON...
STILL?! WHAT STAYS YOU?
BESIDES, HER APPRENTICE-SHIP IS NOT YET FORMAL. THE FIRST TEST AWAITS.
AH, OF COURSE... RIGHT NOW, THE DADAH RANGE MUST BE...
PRECISELY. AT ITS *HIGHEST* ALTITUDE OF THE YEAR.
I CAN'T HAVE HER TAKE IT NOW.
HER VERY LIFE WOULD BE AT RISK.
UM...

ARE YOU...
...SURE ABOUT THIS, AGOTT?
MASTER QIFREY'S AWAY, AND...
IT MAKES NO DIFFERENCE. YOU TEST ALONE.

THE FIRST TEST IS THE "CONSENT OF THE CROWN."
YOU'RE ALLOWED TO TAKE YOUR COMPONENTS AND THREE CONTRAPTIONS. THAT'S IT.
YOU MUST REACH THE HIGHEST PEAK OF THE DADAH RANGE WITHOUT ANYONE'S AID, AND PICK OF THE DIADEM HERB THAT FLOURISHES THERE.

THE THREE CHOSEN TOOLS MUST COME FROM YOUR OWN ABODE AND BE WITHIN YOUR OWN CAPACITY TO USE.
HUH?! SO... I COULD TAKE THE *TOILET* IF I WANTED?!
THE ONE WHERE YOU CAN SEE THE UNIVERSE...?!
THAT ONE USES *VERY* PRECISE MAGIC. YOU CAN'T JUST PICK IT UP AND MOVE IT AROUND.

WE'VE GOT A GUIDANCE ORB THAT SHOWS THE WAY TO ANY DESTINATION, AND THE VAPOR BUBBLE FOR DRINKING WATER.
I IMAGINE THAT'S THE EXTENT OF WHAT YOU CAN HANDLE.

UM... WHAT ABOUT...
...A PAIR OF THOSE SHOES?

WHAT SHOES?

もじ FIDGET
もじ FIDGET
もじ FIDGET
SO...
...IF IT'S NOT A BOTHER, MAYBE YOU COULD...
もじ FIDGET
もじ FIDGET

I SAW THE SOLES GLOWING WHEN YOU AND MASTER QIFREY WERE FLYING AROUND.
THEY'RE CONTRAP-TIONS, TOO, AREN'T THEY?

もじ FIIDGE
I DUNNO, LEND THEM TO ME, OR...
...!

HERE.
!

SORRY, YOU'RE RIGHT! IT WOULDN'T BE FAIR!!
FORGET I ASKED!!

YOU CAN BORROW THEM.
OH...! THANK Y—
SHOVE
SHOVE

NOW HURRY UP AND GET ON WITH IT.
FLING

WHUMP

OH. I ALMOST FORGOT TO TELL YOU...

YOU ONLY GET ONE CHANCE TO TAKE THIS TEST.

IF YOU FAIL, YOU CAN'T BE APPROVED AS MASTER QIFREY'S APPRENTICE.
YOU'LL HAVE TO LEAVE THE ATELIER.

SHWOOM

ドキ
WHUMP

NOW HURRY UP AND GET ON WITH IT.
ポイッ
FLING

OH...! THANK Y—
YOU CAN BORROW THEM.
ぐい
SHOVE
ぐい
SHOVE

YOU ONLY GET ONE CHANCE TO TAKE THIS TEST.

OH. I ALMOST FORGOT TO TELL YOU...

IF YOU FAIL, YOU CAN'T BE APPROVED AS MASTER QIFREY'S APPRENTICE.
YOU'LL HAVE TO LEAVE THE ATELIER.

SHWOOM

...I'M FEELING A LOT LESS CONFIDENT AGAIN.
CLUTCH

BUT I HAVE TO TRY.
THERE'S NO GOING BACK NOW!

THE GUIDANCE ORB SAYS...
TINK
TINK
...TO GO THIS WAY.

ALL RIGHT. IT'S JUST SOME CLIMBING. NO BIG DEAL!
I CAN DO THIS!
FWING
FWING
FWING
IF EVEN A *10-YEAR-OLD* CAN MAKE IT...

RUSTLE
TINK
TINK
...THEN IT MUST BE A PIECE OF CA—

THAT'S THE DADAH RANGE...?

CHAPTER 3 ♦ END

Witch Hat Atelier

IN ORDER TO BECOME AN APPRENTICE, I HAVE TO PICK THE DIADEM HERB...

...WHICH GROWS AT THE TOP OF THE DADAH RANGE.

TA-DAH!

THE SHOES I BORROWED FROM AGOTT!

HALF OF THE SEAL'S ON THE LEFT FOOT, AND HALF ON THE RIGHT.

SO I HAVE TO PUT THEM PERFECTLY TOGETHER...

MASTER QIFREY WAS RIGHT.
I AM LIKE A NEWBORN FOAL...

WOW! THIS IS AMAZING!
OH MY GOSH!
I DON'T BELIEVE IT!
I'M ACTUALLY FLOATING!

WHIP
EEP!

WOBBLE
WHOA!
WAIT!
WOBBLE

RUSTLE
BUT IF I CAN FLY, REACHING THE PEAK WILL BE A BREEZE.
OKAY. TIME TO FIGURE THIS OUT!

...
TEETER
TOTTER

"SOON YOU'LL BE FULL OF CONFI-DENCE."
THINK POSITIVE ...
TEETER
TOTTER
THINK POSITIVE ...

ALL RIGHT! I THINK MY BALANCE IS GETTING BETTER!

TIME TO TRY GOING A LITTLE HIGHER...
ぐら
WOBBLE
ぐら
WOBBLE

AHH!
EEP!
WHOA!
LURCH

し!
AB
はっ
GR

ぷらん
DANGLE

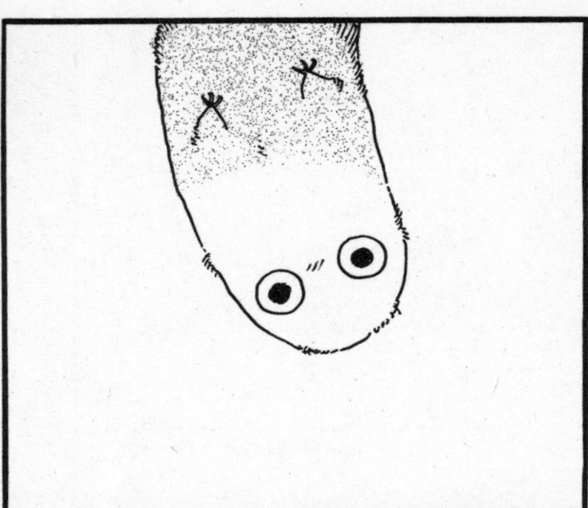

PWEE!

EEEE-
EEK!
FLUMP
ぼてっ

AHHHHHH!!
KER-
SPLASH
...

!

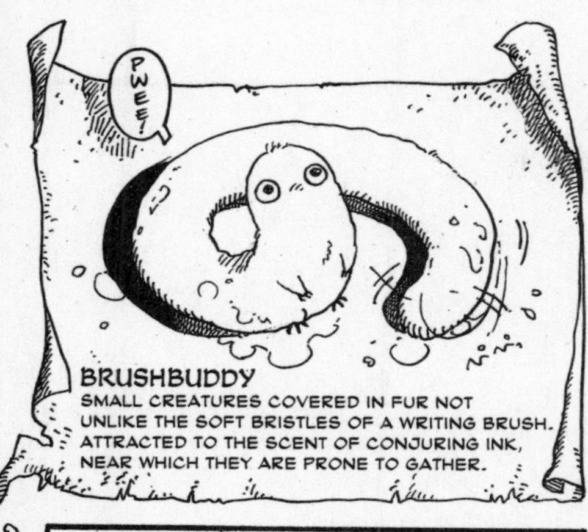
PWEE!
BRUSHBUDDY
SMALL CREATURES COVERED IN FUR NOT UNLIKE THE SOFT BRISTLES OF A WRITING BRUSH. ATTRACTED TO THE SCENT OF CONJURING INK, NEAR WHICH THEY ARE PRONE TO GATHER.

IT'S A BRUSH-BUDDY! I'D NEVER SEEN ONE BEFORE!
IT MUST BE DRAWN TO THE MAGIC I'M USING!

HAAAAAH...
AWW... NOW MY SHOES ARE ALL MUDDY-DUDDY...
SCRUB
SCRUB
SCRUB
SCRUB
SCRUB
SPLISH

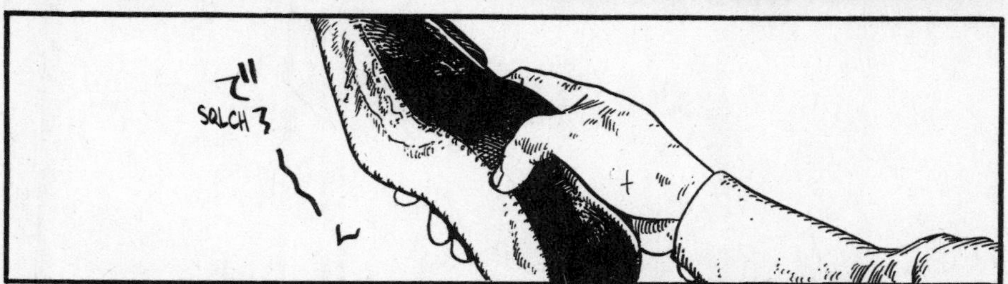
SQLCH

HUH?!
THE SEAL'S RUBBED OFF!

EEEEEP!
NO! IS IT BECAUSE I WIPED IT?!
RUMMAGE
THIS IS NOT GOOD! OKAY, OKAY. I'LL JUST TRACE OVER IT...
RUMMAGE

THE INK...
This is really bad.
THERE'S NO WAY I CAN FIX THIS.
Oh nooo. I don't believe this.
It's leaked over every-thing.

PWEE...

WHAT AM I GONNA DO...?
IS IT OVER FOR ME...?

KRSPLSHH
KRSPLSHH

HERE'S THE APPLICATION FORM.
THANK YOU.
IT'LL BE JUST A MOMENT.

IF YOU LIVED HERE AT THE HALL, YOU WOULDN'T HAVE TO TRAVEL FOR THINGS LIKE THIS...
ROOM ENOUGH FOR YOUR APPRENTICES, TOO.

IT'S THE CENTER OF OUR WORLD.
WITH ACCESS TO EVERYTHING A WITCH COULD EVER NEED.

...YOUR DISDAIN FOR THE HALL RUNS DEEP.

WELL, IF YOU INSIST ON LIVING IN THAT BACKWOODS ATELIER...

...AT LEAST KEEP A CLOSE EYE ON YOUR APPRENTICES.

FOR LITTLE MICE OF THAT AGE...

...THERE'S NO TELLING WHAT GOES ON WHEN THE CAT'S AWAY.

HUH?

HEY, AGOTT...
HAVE YOU SEEN COCO?

YOU WON'T FIND COCO AROUND HERE.
SHE'S AT THE DADAH RANGE, TAKING THE TEST.

IT'S ALMOST TIME FOR DINNER, BUT THERE'S NO ANSWER...
...WHEN I KNOCK ON HER DOOR.
THINK SHE'S ASLEEP?

HUH?!!
SHE'S THERE BY *HERSELF* ?!
ARE YOU SERIOUS ?!
SHE'S JUST BARELY MOVED IN! WHY DIDN'T YOU STOP HER?!

YOU'RE SUPPOSED TO TAKE IT *BEFORE* YOU MOVE IN.
TH... THAT'S TRUE, BUT...

CRACKLE

IF SHE CAN'T PASS A TEST THAT EASY...
...SHE'S NOT FIT TO BE AN APPRENTICE.

I WON'T TOLERATE ANYONE WHO CAN'T KEEP UP WITH ME.
THERE'S NOTHING TO GAIN SPENDING TIME...
...WITH SOMEONE BENEATH ME. *ESPECIALLY* AN OUT-SIDER.

...
STOP WORRYING. SHE'LL COME RIGHT BACK WITHOUT EVEN TRYING.

SHE'S OBLIVIOUS. NO SENSE OF DANGER. NO GRASP OF HOW THINGS WORK.

THE RANGE IS SATURATED WITH MOISTURE. IT'S AS HIGH AS IT GETS ALL YEAR.
NOT EVEN SYLPH SHOES CAN MAKE IT TO THE TOP.

KRSHH

SHE SHOULDN'T BE A PART OF OUR WORLD.

HAAAH...
I TRIED TO FIX THE SHOES WITH WHAT INK I HAD LEFT...
BUT THEY WON'T EVEN ACTIVATE ANYMORE.

UGH, IT'S NO USE...

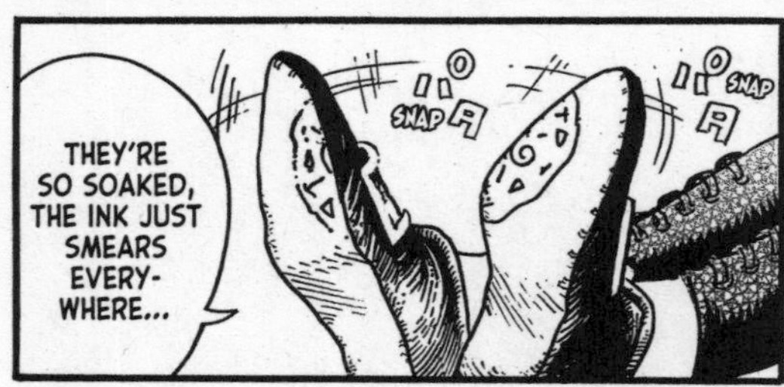
SNAP
SNAP
THEY'RE SO SOAKED, THE INK JUST SMEARS EVERY-WHERE...

MAYBE IF I DREW IT ON THE SOLES OF MY FEET...?

NO. I CAN'T.
DRAWING MAGIC DIRECTLY ON THE BODY IS FORBIDDEN.

GULP

I DON'T EVEN KNOW...
...WHAT OTHER KINDS OF SPELLS THERE ARE TO TURN TO AT A TIME LIKE THIS...

FLOP

PWEE
SLINK

JOLT
THUD

AGOTT WAS RIGHT ALL ALONG.

JUST BECAUSE ANYONE CAN DRAW MAGIC...
...DOESN'T MEAN THAT IT'S EASY TO DRAW WELL.

I GUESS...
...REGULAR FOLK REALLY DON'T HAVE WHAT IT TAKES.

PIGMENT STONE
A STONE USED BY TAILORS TO MARK OUT PATTERNS ON CLOTH.

バッ
FWISH
サッ

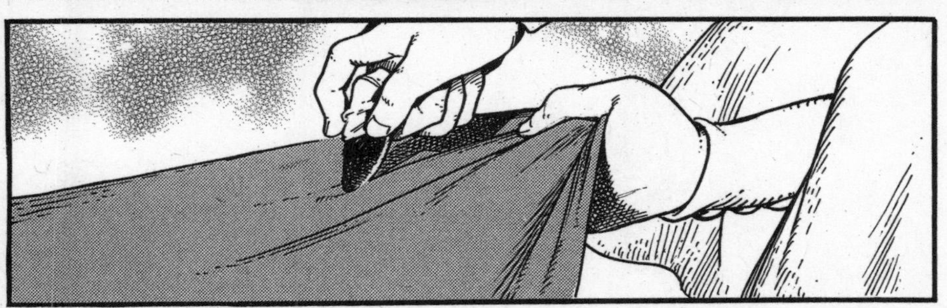

"EVERYONE'S UNSTEADY WHEN FIRST USING A NEW TOOL."

IF THAT'S HOW IT IS...

...THEN I'LL JUST SWITCH TO A TOOL I AM USED TO.

AND MY FINGERS ...
...WILL BE FREE TO DANCE AS THEY PLEASE.
PER-FECTLY FREE.

CHIRP CHIRP
ピチチチ…
CHIRP CHIRP
ピチチチ…
READY TO GO!
TUG!
FLUTTER
パタタタ
FLUTTER
MORNING, LITTLE BRUSH-BUDDY!
YOU'RE NOT SHY AT ALL, ARE YOU?

SO I DECIDED TO TRY USING JUST *ONE* AND MADE IT *REALLY* LONG!
TA-
DAH

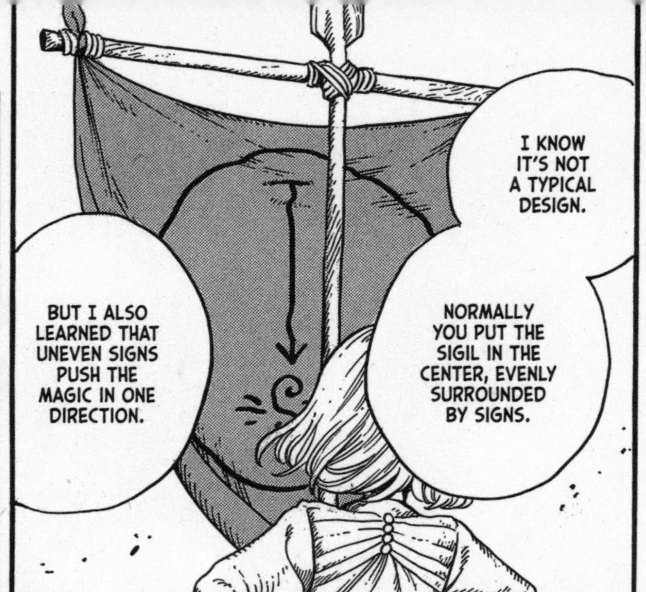
I KNOW IT'S NOT A TYPICAL DESIGN.
NORMALLY YOU PUT THE SIGIL IN THE CENTER, EVENLY SURROUNDED BY SIGNS.
BUT I ALSO LEARNED THAT UNEVEN SIGNS PUSH THE MAGIC IN ONE DIRECTION.

YOU WANT TO COME ALONG?
PWEE!
ALL RIGHT...

!

I HAVE NO IDEA IF THIS IS GONNA WORK...

SHHK
...BUT BE SURE TO HANG ON TIGHT!
'CAUSE HERE GOES NOTHING!

VWOOSH
PLICK!
スポッ!

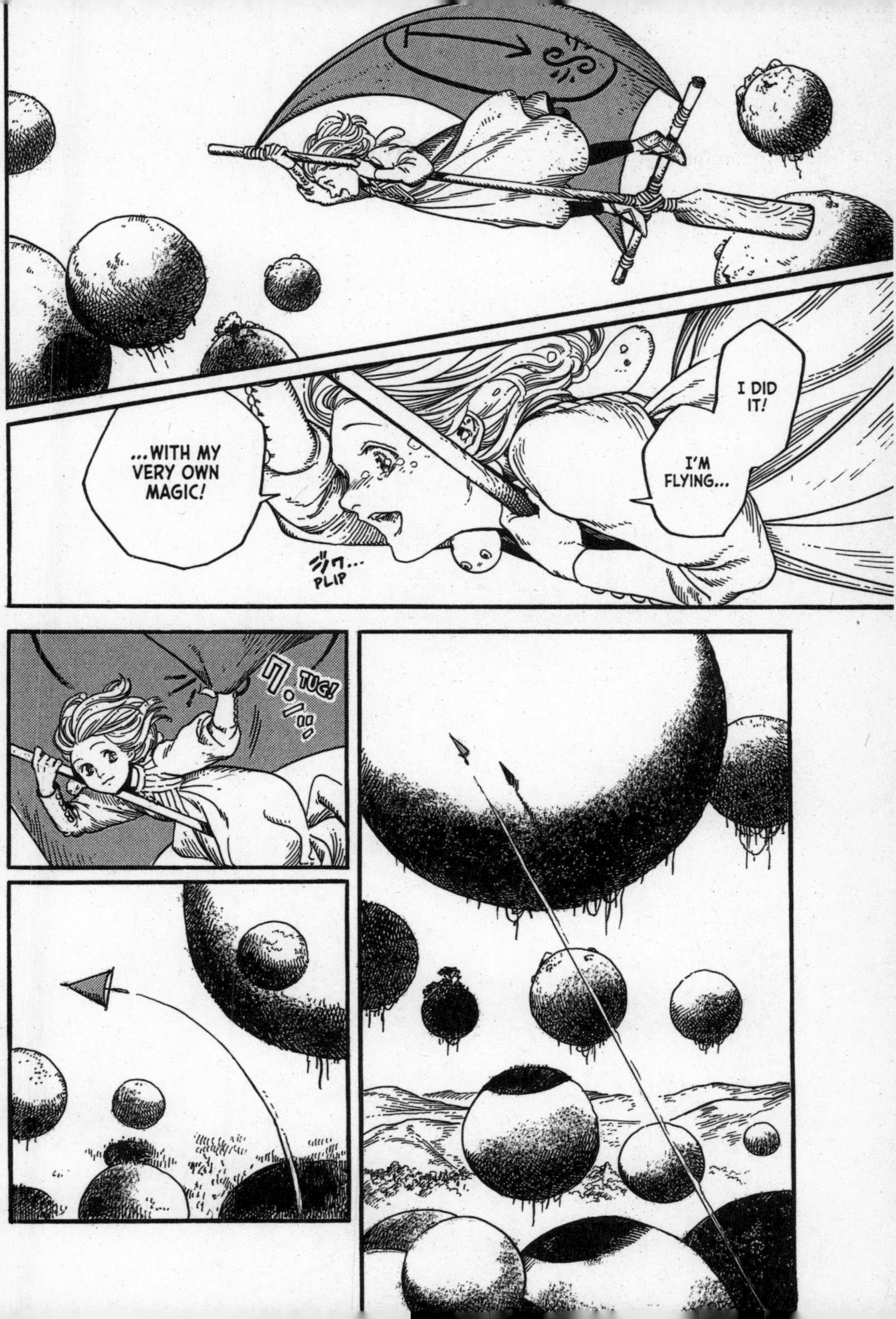

I DID IT!
I'M FLYING...
...WITH MY VERY OWN MAGIC!
PLIP

...
IT'S A DREAM COME TRUE. A REAL, LIVE CLOAK OF FLIGHT!
IN THE END, IT WAS THE THINGS I LEARNED WHILE HELPING MOM...
...THAT SHOWED ME THE WAY TO USE MAGIC.
WAIT FOR ME, MOM. I'LL BE BACK FOR YOU.

I PROMISE TO FIX...
ボ
PW
フムッ
OOF!

...THE MISTAKE I MADE!

AH, TETIA. I'M BACK.
MASTER QIFREY!
IT'S COCO! SHE'S...!
THUD

YOU MEAN...
...SHE'S GONE BY HERSELF...
...TO TAKE THE TEST?!
NOD
NOD

IT'S FAR TOO RISKY!
WE HAVE TO STOP HER!
BUT SHE'LL *FAIL* IF WE...

SHE SHOULDN'T BE THERE AT ALL! IT'S TOO SOON!
SHE'S NOT LIKE US! SHE'S ONLY JUST ENTERED OUR WORLD!

IF SOMETHING HAPPENS TO COCO...
...IT'S NOT ONLY THE GIRL WE'LL LOSE!

GRRR
KK

OKAY. THAT'S THE RIGHT SETTING...

HUH?

COCO!

I GOT THE CONSENT OF THE CROWN.

...

HERE'S MY PROOF. THIS MEANS I DID IT, RIGHT?

くるっ
TWIRL

...COCO...
...!

...

USING MAGIC WITHOUT SUFFICIENT UNDERSTANDING...
...AND CAREFUL PREPARATION IS A VERY RECKLESS THING TO DO.
YOU OF ALL PEOPLE SHOULD KNOW THAT.
SLUMP
しゅん...
AND, QUITE FRANKLY...
...THERE WAS NO NEED TO BRAVE DANGER TO PROVE YOURSELF.
LIFT
A SINGLE MISSTEP COULD HAVE BEEN FATAL.
YOU MUST NEVER BEHAVE LIKE THIS AGAIN.
I'M SORRY, MASTER QIFREY...

YOU ARE ALREADY MY APPRENTICE.

IS THIS...?!

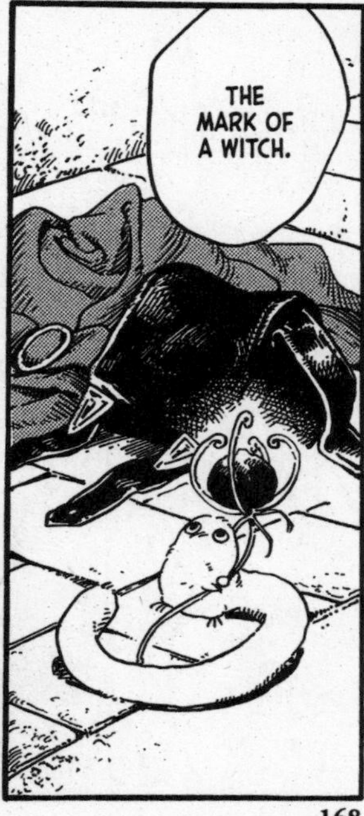
THE MARK OF A WITCH.

A SYMBOL OF PRIDE ...
...YET ALSO OF YOUR SOLEMN VOW...
...NEVER TO USE MAGIC FOR VILE PURPOSES.
LET ITS WEIGHT EVER REMIND OF THE RESPONSIBILITY YOU BEAR.

FOR THAT POINTED CAP...

...SHALL BE WATCHING OVER YOU AND YOUR MAGIC.

SO THE SEED HAS SPROUTED.

CHAPTER 4 ♦ END

Witch Hat Atelier

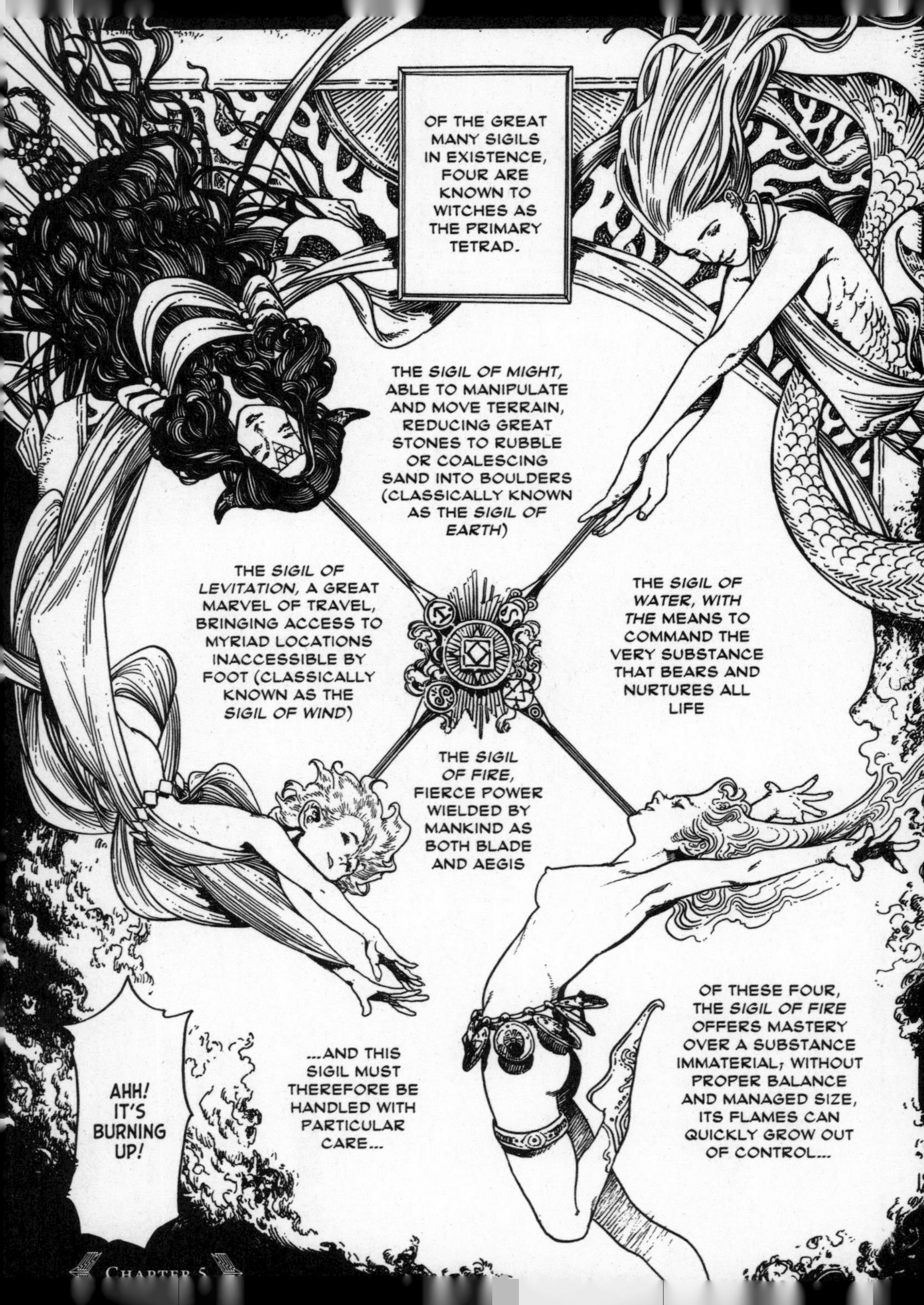
OF THE GREAT MANY SIGILS IN EXISTENCE, FOUR ARE KNOWN TO WITCHES AS THE PRIMARY TETRAD.
THE *SIGIL OF MIGHT*, ABLE TO MANIPULATE AND MOVE TERRAIN, REDUCING GREAT STONES TO RUBBLE OR COALESCING SAND INTO BOULDERS (CLASSICALLY KNOWN AS THE *SIGIL OF EARTH*)
THE *SIGIL OF WATER, WITH THE* MEANS TO COMMAND THE VERY SUBSTANCE THAT BEARS AND NURTURES ALL LIFE
THE *SIGIL OF LEVITATION*, A GREAT MARVEL OF TRAVEL, BRINGING ACCESS TO MYRIAD LOCATIONS INACCESSIBLE BY FOOT (CLASSICALLY KNOWN AS THE *SIGIL OF WIND*)
THE *SIGIL OF FIRE*, FIERCE POWER WIELDED BY MANKIND AS BOTH BLADE AND AEGIS
OF THESE FOUR, THE *SIGIL OF FIRE* OFFERS MASTERY OVER A SUBSTANCE IMMATERIAL; WITHOUT PROPER BALANCE AND MANAGED SIZE, ITS FLAMES CAN QUICKLY GROW OUT OF CONTROL...
...AND THIS SIGIL MUST THEREFORE BE HANDLED WITH PARTICULAR CARE...
AHH! IT'S BURNING UP!

ざば
KSPLLLSH
SZZL!

A-ARE YOU OKAY?

THANKS, TETIA.
WOBBLE WOBBLE ヨロリ ヨロ…
AND THANK *YOU!*
SO... WHAT WERE YOU UP TO, ANYWAY?

I WAS DRAWING FIRE MAGIC.

"ON ITS OWN, FIRE MAGIC WILL CONSUME THE PAPER AND THE SEAL ITSELF..."
"...BUT FIRE SUSPENDED IN *AIR* WILL BURN ON. THE PERFECT EXERCISE TO PRACTICE LEVITATION MAGIC!"
THAT'S WHAT MASTER QIFREY SAID, BUT...
SOLCH じゃば

WHY ARE YOU HUNG UP ON LEVITATION MAGIC?

YOU CONQUERED THE DADAH RANGE!

BOB

BOB

YOU FLEW ALL OVER THE PLACE, LIKE *WHOOSH*...

...*FWOOSH*... ACROSS THE SKY, DIDN'T YOU?!

FWOOOOOSH

ちょばばばびゅーん

WHEN I WAS OUT THERE, I RUINED AGOTT'S SYLPH SHOES.

I WANTED TO FIX THEM UP BEFORE I RETURNED THEM...

WHOA! DID YOU DO THIS?! THEY LOOK BRAND NEW!
WE USED TO REPAIR TRAVELERS' SHOES AT HOME...

ALL THAT'S LEFT IS TO REDRAW THE SEAL.
BUT MY LINES ALWAYS COME OUT ALL THIN AND WAVY...

LEAN
PERHAPS WE NEED TO FIND YOU A NEW WAND.
!

THE ONE YOU HAVE NOW IS JUST ONE OF MY OWN OLD WANDS.
IT REALLY IS QUITE IMPOR-TANT...
...TO HAVE A PEN WHOSE WEIGHT AND GRIP SUITS YOU.

I SUPPOSE WE OUGHT TO HAVE YOU TRY A FEW AND SELECT FOR YOURSELF.
ALL RIGHT! THEN IT'S DECIDED.

WE'LL TAKE A TRIP TO THE STATIONER'S.
THE *MAGIC* STATIONER'S!

THERE'S ...
THERE'S A *SHOP* LIKE THAT...?!

THE *STATIONER'S!* EVEN THE *NAME* IS LOVELY...!
UM... COCO?
Oh, wow!
Oh, it sounds so great...!
JUST A MOMENT! I'M STILL SAVORING THE WORDS...!

KALHN, TOWNSHIP OF THE MARSHWOODS

WOW!

JUST SO. KALHN IS THE LARGEST SETTLEMENT OF WITCHES IN OUR AREA.

THERE ARE SO MANY WITCHES HERE!

WITCHES BUILT UP THIS SHOAL IN THE MIDDLE OF THE RIVER TO SUPPORT A GREAT WATCHTOWER...

...MEANT TO PROTECT THE TOWN FROM MOLEWYRMS INHABITING THE MARSHWOODS ON THE OPPOSITE BANK.

WITCHES FLOCKED HERE, AND SOON IT WAS FULL OF ATELIERS.

CLASSROOM MODE

THEY NEVER EVEN BUILT A BRIDGE. NO ONE NEEDED IT!

WOW...

MASTER QIFREY...

I THINK COCO'S LEFT CLASS.

I'D RATHER NOT SPEND MY TIME PLAYING TOUR GUIDE FOR COCO.

THERE ARE SOME SHOPS I'D LIKE TO VISIT...

...SO I'M GOING ON AHEAD.

I'LL MEET YOU AT THE STATIONER'S BEFORE IT'S TIME TO GO HOME. IS THAT ALL RIGHT?

I... SUPPOSE.

SEE YOU THEN.

I'D LIKE TO BE FRIENDS WITH HER IF I CAN.

THAT TIME I CAUGHT A GLIMPSE OF HER DRAWING...

...HER LINES WERE SO PRECISE, AND HER SEALS SO LOVELY.

CHATTER
ガャ
BUSTLE
ワィ
BUSTLE
ワィ
BUSTLE
ワィ
CHATTER
ガャ
ガャ
CHATTER

GASP!

COCO? WHAT'S WRONG?

OH, UM... IT'S NOTHING.
MUST'VE IMAGINED THAT... RIGHT?

UP HERE, COCO!

COME IN AND SEE.
WELCOME TO "THE STARRY SWORD"...
STATIONER EXTRAORDI-NAIRE.

WHOA...

THERE'S A HUGE TREE RIGHT INSIDE THE SHOP.

WELL, I'LL BE... AN APPRENTICE GAWKIN' AT A SILVERWOOD?

HAVEN'T YOU EVER SEEN ONE? IT DON'T GET MORE BASIC THAN THAT.

PLEASE EXCUSE COCO.
SHE ONLY RECENTLY BECAME AN APPRENTICE, MISTER NOLNOA.

WELL, THAT EXPLAINS IT!
AHA HA HA!
'COURSE YOU'D BE GAWKIN'! SORRY, LITTLE MISS.

LEAN
HO! IS THAT SO?
THEN *THIS* GIRL MUST BE THE...

YOU DIDN'T RECOGNIZE MY TREE, AND I DIDN'T RECOGNIZE YOU! S'POSE THAT MAKES US EVEN!

THIS IS MISTER NOLNOA, COCO.
HE OWNS THIS SHOP, *THE STARRY SWORD!*

THAT'S RIGHT!
ALL THE COMPONENTS YOU'LL FIND HERE WERE CRAFTED BY ME 'N' MY GRANDSON, TARTAH!
EVERY KIND OF WAND AND INK UNDER THE SUN. EVEN DO CUSTOM EXTRACTIONS ...
...AT WHATEVER CONCEN-TRATION YOU NEED!

"EXTRAC-TIONS"...?
?

QIFREY, MY LAD, YOU BEEN SPENDIN' TOO MUCH TIME AWAY FROM THE CLASSROOM?
A FINE HEAD OF HAIR AND SCHOLARLY GOOD LOOKS AIN'T NO EXCUSE! A TEACHER'S GOTTA TEACH!
AS I SAID, SHE ONLY RECENTLY BEGAN...
"Scholarly good looks"...?

WELL, FOR YOU, COCO, I'LL PROVIDE A DEMONSTRATION. FOLLOW ME.
O-OKAY!

SHKT
SHKT
SHKT
?

...

YOU COMIN'?
YES!

YOU'RE IN LUCK! THIS BRANCH HAS BLACKENED UP REAL NICE.

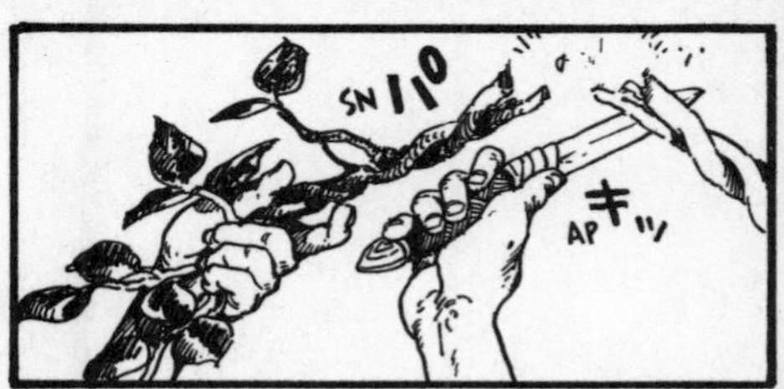
SN
AP

NOW WATCH CLOSELY.
PLUNK

THAT, COCO, IS WOODCRUOR.
REALLY?!

IT GOT ALL DARK!

SEEP

LEFT LIKE THAT, THEY'RE POISONOUS. TO THE TREE, 'N' TO PEOPLE, TOO.
DRAIN ONE OUT IN BOILIN' WATER, SIPHON OFF THE EXCESS AND...
BLUP

WHEN THE HEALTHY, SILVER-WHITE BRANCHES WITHER, THEY GO BLACK AS COAL.

COMMONPLACE INK IS MADE BY BURNING WOOD AND COLLECTING SOOT LEFT BY THE SMOKE.
BUT CONJURING INK IS DIFFERENT.

...PRESTO, THE ROOT OF MAGIC ITSELF—RAW INK, READY TO REFINE.
SPLISH

AS THE NAME "WOODCRUOR" IMPLIES...

...WE HARVEST THE "BLOOD" OF THE SILVER-WOOD.

AND THUS THE TREE IS OF SPECIAL IMPORT TO WITCHES.

RIGHT! CAN'T GET INK FROM ANY OTHER TREE, STRANGE AS IT SEEMS.

THERE'S AN OLD LEGEND THAT A SILVERWOOD ONCE FELL IN LOVE WITH A WITCH...

... AND OFFERED UP ITS BRANCHES AS WANDS AND CRUOR AS INK...

OH, THAT'S RIGHT! A WAND!

WELL, NOW...
...IS THAT WHAT BROUGHT YOU IN TODAY? WAND SHOPPING?
THAT'S RIGHT.
THEN I S'POSE YOU'LL NEED A BIT OF THIS TO TRY A FEW OUT.

I'M SURE THERE'S ONE DOWN THERE THAT'S PERFECT FOR YOU, LITTLE MISS.

BY THE WAY, MISTER NOLNOA, I WONDER IF YOU MIGHT ORDER IN SOME PAPER FOR ME.
WE'LL BE DOWN-STAIRS IN THE SHOP, MASTER!
LET'S GO, COCO!
OKAY!

WHAT KIND OF WAND ARE YOU GONNA GET?
I LIKE THE ONE YOU HAVE, TETIA. IT'S SO LIGHT AND...

W...
ダッ!
DASH
WAIT!

COCO?!

I'M LOOKING FOR SOLES FOR SYLPH SHOES.
SOMETHING IN MY SIZE. PREFERABLY NOT OF WOOD...

AGOTT!
DID COCO COME BY HERE?!
WHAT'S *THAT* ABOUT?

TMP TMP
HUH?!

HEY, WHAT'RE YOU...?!
WE'VE GOTTA CATCH UP!
COME ON, AGOTT!

WHY DO *I* HAVE TO GO...?!

DID SOMETHING HAPPEN?
NO IDEA...
SHE JUST SPED OFF.
PANT
PANT

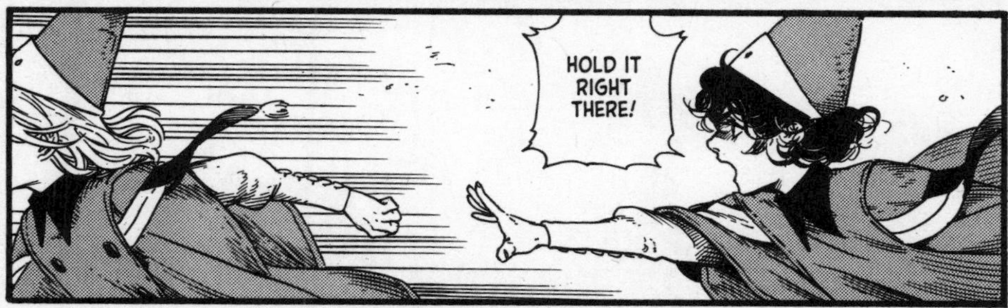
HOLD IT RIGHT THERE!

BILLOW
COCO! WAIT UP!

FWSH...

WHAT DO YOU THINK YOU'RE DOING?!
WHERE ARE YOU RUNNING OFF TO?!

!

TH-THAT WITCH WAS THERE! IN FRONT OF THE SHOP!
THE ONE WHO SOLD ME THE BOOK OF FORBIDDEN SPELLS!

ALWAYS CAUSING A FUSS...
AT LEAST WE'RE TOGETHER! LET'S GET BACK...
...TO THE SHOP.
...I WAS TOO SLOW.

PAUSE...

HEY...

...DOESN'T THIS PLACE SEEM *REALLY* DIFFERENT FOR BEING...
...JUST ONE ALLEY OFF THE MAIN ROAD?

HUH ...?
AND LOOK AROUND ...

...THE ARCHITECTURE HAS COMPLETELY CHANGED.

I WAS SO FOCUSED ON RUNNING, I GUESS I GOT US ALL LOST.
BUT WE CAN'T BE TOO FAR AWAY, RIGHT?
HUH? SO WHERE ARE WE?
AND...UM... WHICH WAY DID WE COME FROM?
FWP

KALHN DOESN'T HAVE ROADS AND WALLS OF WHITE STONE LIKE THIS...

TH...
THAT'S SILLY! WE DIDN'T PASS THROUGH ANY WINDOW-WAY...
...AND IT'S NOT LIKE WE *TELEPORTED!*
WE JUST GOT TURNED AROUND! THAT'S ALL!

ARE WE NOT IN KALHN ANYMORE?

THAT WE JUST GOT TURNED AROUND?
NO, NOT THAT.

...SHE MIGHT HAVE A POINT.

I'LL GO CHECK WHERE WE ARE FROM ABOVE!
TETIA, WAIT!

...SPELLS LIKE THAT ARE *FORBIDDEN*...

WE COULD HAVE BEEN TELEPORTED DIRECTLY. WITHOUT OUR KNOWLEDGE.

BUT... I THOUGHT THAT WASN'T ALLOWED?
MASTER QIFREY SAID...

EEEEEEK!!
!!

TETIA?! WHAT'S WRONG?!

BAD NEWS! *REALLY* BAD NEWS!
WE ARE *DEFINITELY* NOT IN KALHN ANYMORE!!
AB
GR
WE'VE GOTTA GET OUT OF HERE! RUN!!

WAIT! TETIA, SLOW DOWN!
TMP TMP TMP TMP TMP TMP TMP TMP TMP TMP
DID YOU SEE SOME-THING?

IT'S NOT JUST THAT *I* SAW *IT*!
IT SAW *ME*!!

WHAT'RE YOU TAL—

MISTER NOLNOA!

OF COURSE NOT! THIS SHOP IS THE MOST FASCINATING PLACE IN THE WORLD FOR THEM!
They'd spend all day in here!!
OH, YOU SILVER-TONGUED SCAMP. ♡

MY APPREN-TICES!
HAVE YOU SEEN THEM?! I CAN'T FIND THEM ANY-WHERE!
HM? THEY GET BORED AND WANDER OFF?

I SAW THEM.

IT'S MOST UNLIKE THEM TO LEAVE WITHOUT THANKING YOU.
WHERE COULD THEY HAVE...

THEY WERE CHASING AFTER A WITCH IN SOME WEIRD GARB.
THE WITCH HAD...
...A MASK IN THE SHAPE OF AN EYEBALL...

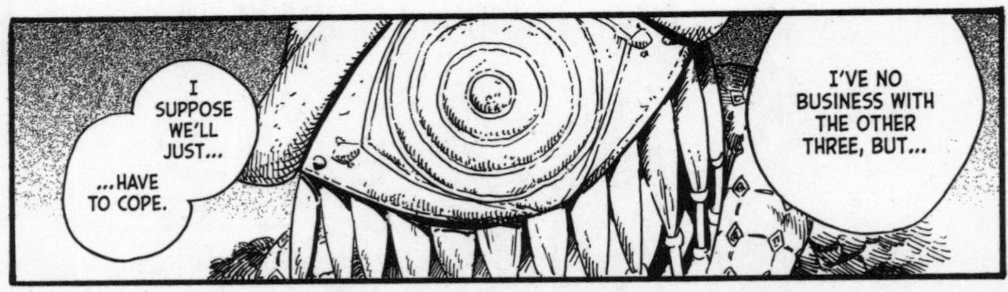

I'VE NO BUSINESS WITH THE OTHER THREE, BUT...
I SUPPOSE WE'LL JUST... ...HAVE TO COPE.

NONETHELESS...
WELCOME, COCO... TO THE WORLD OF MAGIC.

YOU ARE OUR...
...ONE AND ONLY HOPE.
Witch Hat Atelier, Volume 1 ♦ End

AN INTRODUCTION TO CASTING SEALS

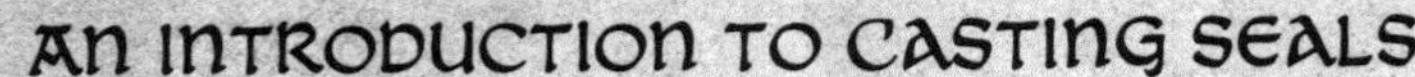

A HANDY REFERENCE ON THE BASIC DESIGNS OF AND RULES FOR CONSTRUCTING MAGIC SEALS.

THE THREE ELEMENTS OF A SEAL

OCCUPIES THE CENTER OF THE SEAL AND DETERMINES THE TYPE OF SPELL CAST.

ARRANGED AROUND THE SIGIL TO INFLUENCE THE FORM, SIZE, AND DIRECTION OF THE SPELL.

ENCOMPASSES THE SIGIL AND SIGNS. COMPLETING THE RING ACTIVATES THE SPELL.

EXAMPLES

SIGIL OF WIND

SIGIL OF WIND UNDERFOOT

SIGIL OF WATER

EXAMPLES

SIGN OF LEVITATION

SIGN OF COLUMNS

SIGN OF CONVERGENCE

EXAMPLES OF CASTING SEALS

SEAL USED ON SYLPH SHOES

BRINGING BOTH HALVES OF THIS SEAL TOGETHER GRANTS STABLE FLIGHT, ENABLING THE USER TO SOAR THROUGH THE SKY.

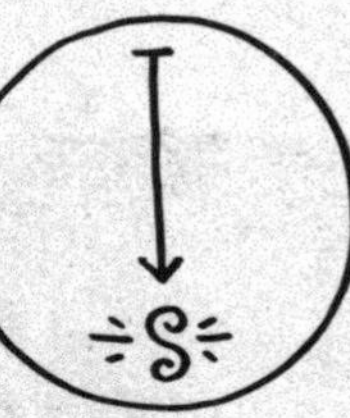

COCO'S SEAL AT THE DADAH RANGE

THE SIGIL IN THIS SEAL IS OFF-CENTER, INFLUENCED BY A SINGLE, EXTREMELY LONG SIGN. IT PRODUCED A VERY POWERFUL AND SHORT-LIVED GUST OF WIND.

A SINGLE SIGN DRAWN LONGER THAN THE OTHERS CAUSED THE SPELL TO DRENCH AGOTT IN WATER. INCIDENTALLY, MASTER QIFREY IS PARTICULARLY SKILLED WITH WATER MAGIC, ENABLING HIM TO CAST MARVELS SUCH AS THE FLOWER MADE OF WATER.

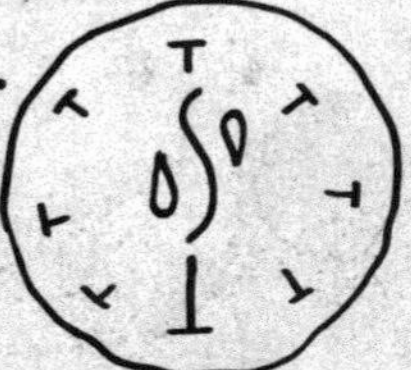

COCO'S VERY FIRST SEAL

THIS SEAL RESULTED IN A SMALL, FLICKERING LIGHT. AS IT WAS COPIED FROM THE BOOK OF FORBIDDEN SPELLS, ITS INTENDED EFFECT IS UNKNOWN.

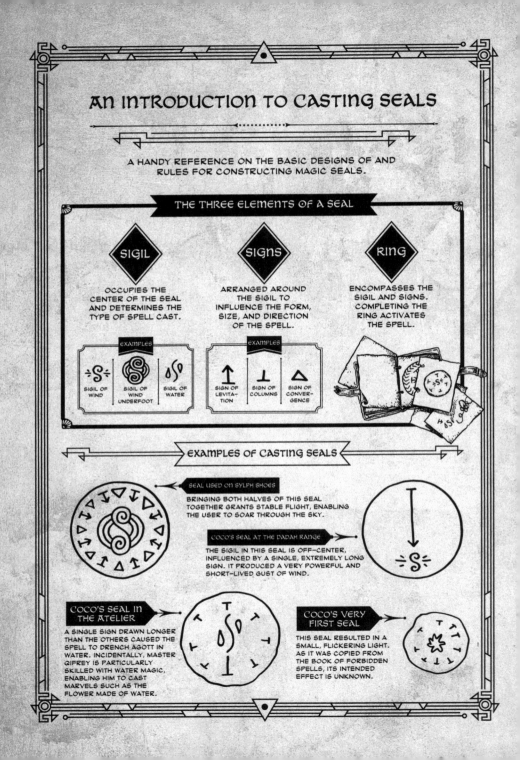

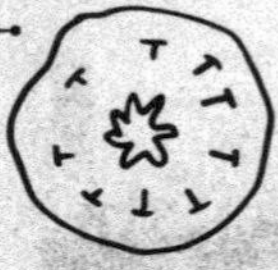

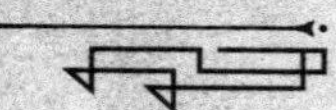

THE WORLD OF *WITCH HAT ATELIER*

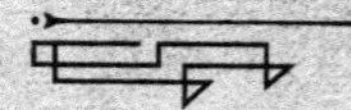

A BRIEF INTRODUCTION OF THE WORLD INHABITED BY COCO AND HER FRIENDS.

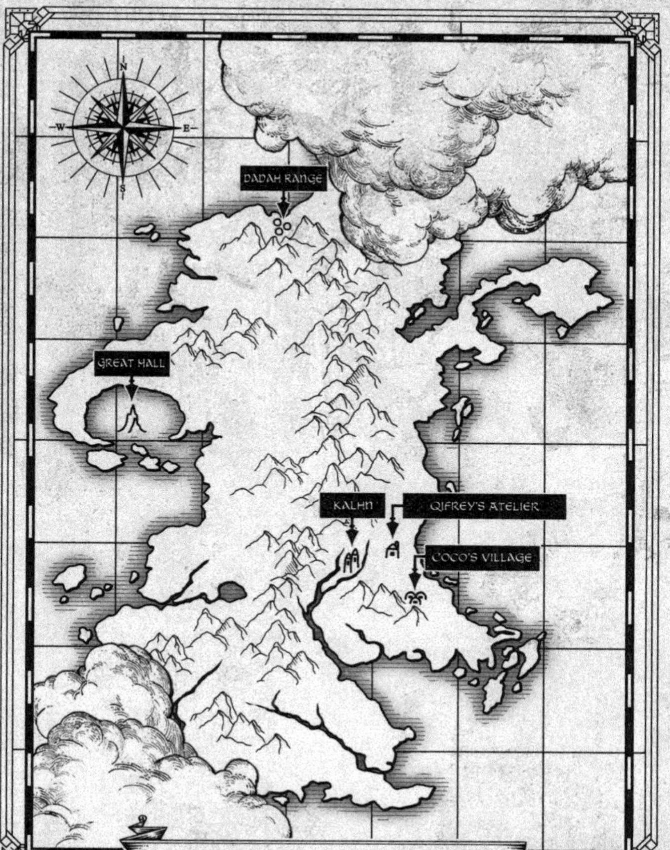

N
W
E
S
DADAH RANGE
GREAT HALL
KALHN
QIFREY'S ATELIER
COCO'S VILLAGE

MAP OF *WITCH HAT*

COCO'S VILLAGE

A SMALL, RURAL VILLAGE NESTLED IN THE FOOTHILLS. CONTRAPTIONS ARE NOT UNHEARD OF HERE, BUT NEITHER ARE THEY FOUND IN GREAT NUMBER. COCO'S HOME INCLUDES A TAILORING SHOP, WHERE COCO HAS HELPED OUT SINCE SHE WAS VERY YOUNG.

QIFREY'S ATELIER

A SINGLE, LONELY BUILDING FOUND A SHORT WAY FROM COCO'S VILLAGE. MANY WITCHES CHOOSE TO TAKE UP RESIDENCE IN THE GREAT HALL, BUT QIFREY PREFERS TO LIVE IN THE COUNTRYSIDE FOR REASONS UNKNOWN.

GREAT HALL

A MASSIVE STRUCTURE POPULATED BY POWERFUL WITCHES. IT LIES AT THE BOTTOM OF THE SEA AND CAN ONLY BE ACCESSED BY DESCENDING A DEEP STAIRWELL WHOSE ENTRANCE IS LOCATED ABOVE THE WAVES.

DADAH RANGE

THE LOCATION OF THE TEST ONE MUST PASS TO BECOME AN APPRENTICE. AN ANCIENT SPELL CAST THERE KEEPS THE MOUNTAINS SUSPENDED IN AIR. THE EXCLUSIVE HABITAT OF THE DIADEM HERB, NEEDED AS PROOF OF COMPLETING THE TEST.

KALHN

A TOWN OF WITCHES, EASILY ACCESSIBLE FROM QIFREY'S ATELIER. PART OF THE TOWN IS BUILT ATOP AN ISLAND, HOME EXCLUSIVELY TO ARTISANS OF MAGIC TOOLS AND OTHERS ENGAGED IN THE USE OF MAGIC.

ARE ONLY THE CHOSEN ABLE TO USE MAGIC ...?
Tetia and Agott's unease about the girls' new plight quickly slips to anger. As Coco witnesses the change in attitude, she's plagued with guilt for wrapping her new friends up in this dire situation. Was it a mistake for an Outsider to try to learn to wield magic? The four apprentices search desperately for answers, but time is running thin.
VOLUME 2: ON SALE IN SUMMER 2019!

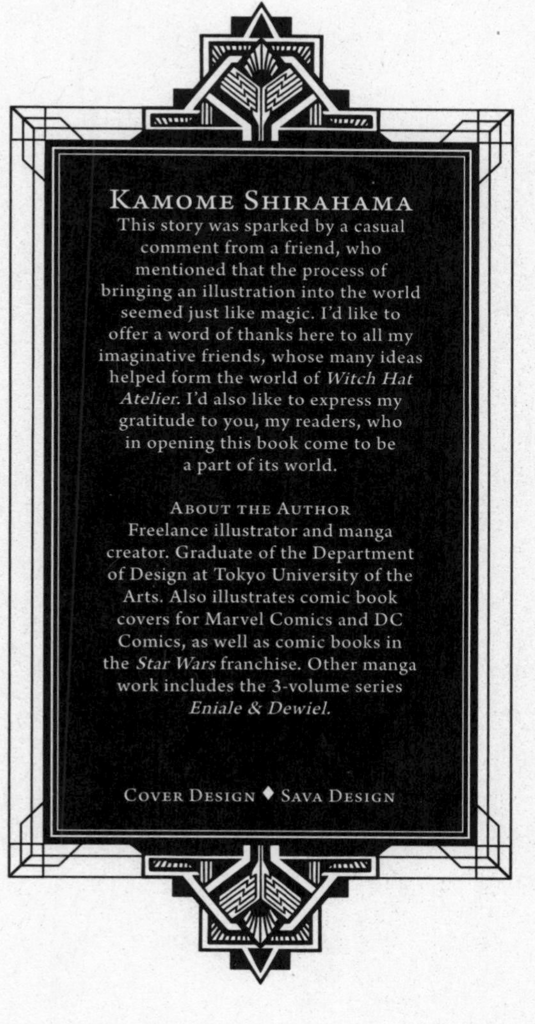

Kamome Shirahama

This story was sparked by a casual comment from a friend, who mentioned that the process of bringing an illustration into the world seemed just like magic. I'd like to offer a word of thanks here to all my imaginative friends, whose many ideas helped form the world of *Witch Hat Atelier*. I'd also like to express my gratitude to you, my readers, who in opening this book come to be a part of its world.

About the Author

Freelance illustrator and manga creator. Graduate of the Department of Design at Tokyo University of the Arts. Also illustrates comic book covers for Marvel Comics and DC Comics, as well as comic books in the *Star Wars* franchise. Other manga work includes the 3-volume series *Eniale & Dewiel.*

Cover Design ♦ Sava Design

Having lost his wife, high school teacher Kōhei Inuzuka is doing his best to raise his young daughter Tsumugi as a single father. He's pretty bad at cooking and doesn't have a huge appetite to begin with, but chance brings his little family together with one of his students, the lonely Kotori. The three of them are anything but comfortable in the kitchen, but the healing power of home cooking might just work on their grieving hearts.

"This season's number-one feel-good anime!" —Anime News Network

"A beautifully-drawn story about comfort food and family and grief. Recommended." —Otaku USA Magazine

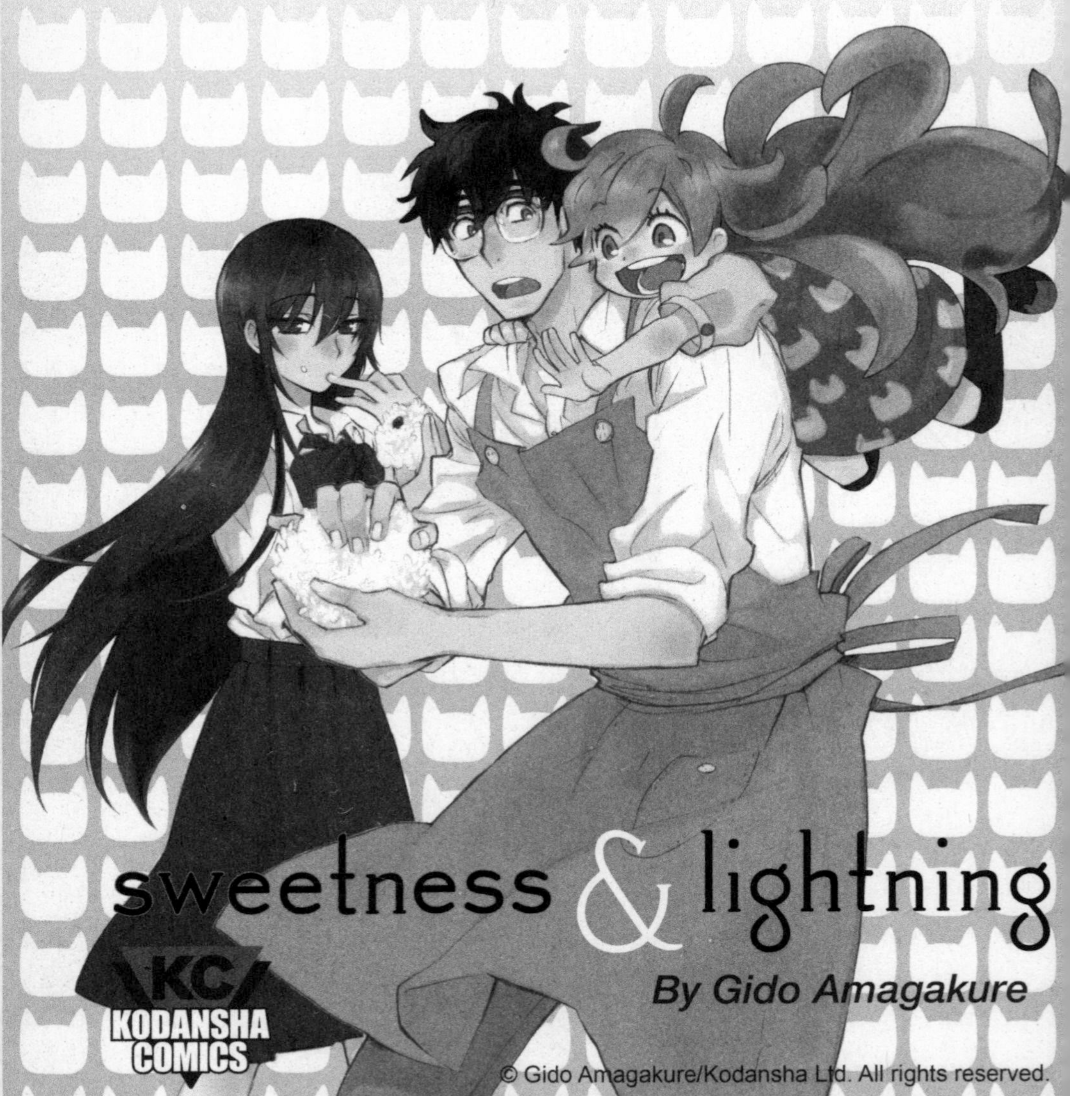

17 years after the original *Cardcaptor Sakura* manga ended, CLAMP returns with more magical adventures from a beloved manga classic!

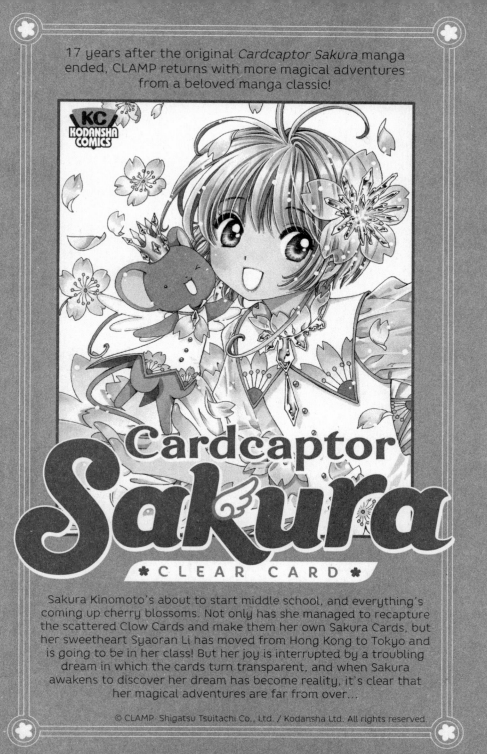

Sakura Kinomoto's about to start middle school, and everything's coming up cherry blossoms. Not only has she managed to recapture the scattered Clow Cards and make them her own Sakura Cards, but her sweetheart Syaoran Li has moved from Hong Kong to Tokyo and is going to be in her class! But her joy is interrupted by a troubling dream in which the cards turn transparent, and when Sakura awakens to discover her dream has become reality, it's clear that her magical adventures are far from over...

Pretty Guardian Sailor Moon

Eternal Edition

The sailor-suited guardians return in this definitive edition of the greatest magical girl manga of all time! Featuring all-new cover illustrations by creator Naoko Takeuchi, a glittering holographic coating, an extra-large size, premium paper, French flaps, and a newly-revised translation!

Teenager Usagi is not the best athlete, she's never gotten good grades, and, well, she's a bit of a crybaby. But when she meets a talking cat, she begins a journey that will teach her she has a well of great strength just beneath the surface, and the heart to inspire and stand up for her friends as Sailor Moon! Experience the *Sailor Moon* manga as never before in these extra-long editions!

Witch Hat Atelier volume 1 is a work of fiction. Names, characters, places, and incidents are the products of the author's imagination or are used fictitiously. Any resemblance to actual events, locales, or persons, living or dead, is entirely coincidental.

A Kodansha Comics Trade Paperback Original.

Published in the United States by Kodansha Comics, an imprint of Kodansha USA Publishing, LLC, New York.

Publication rights for this English edition arranged through Kodansha Ltd., Tokyo.

First published in Japan in 2017 by Kodansha Ltd., Tokyo, as *Tongari Bōshi no Atorie* volume 1.

ISBN 978-1-63236-770-9

Printed in the United States of America.

www.kodanshacomics.com

9 8 7 6 5 4 3 2 1

Translation: Stephen Kohler
Lettering: Lys Blakeslee
Editing: Ajani Oloye
Kodansha Comics edition cover design: Phil Balsman